WE'RE NOT DEAD YET

MILLY WALSH AND JOHN CALLAN

WE'RE
NOT DEAD
YET

THE FIRST WORLD WAR DIARY
OF PRIVATE BERT COOKE

Vanwell Publishing Limited

St. Catharines, Ontario

Vanwell Publishing acknowledges the financial support of the Government of Canada through the Book Publishing Industry Development Program for our publishing activities.

Vanwell Publishing acknowledges the Government of Ontario through the Ontario Media Development Corporation's Book Initiative.

Design: Linda Moroz-Irvine
Cover: Private Bert Cooke

Vanwell Publishing Limited
1 Northrup Crescent
P.O. Box 2131
St. Catharines, Ontario L2R 7S2
sales@vanwell.com
1-800-661-6136

For sales in the United States, please contact Casemate Publishing at 610-853-9131 or
    casemate@casematepublishing.com.
For sales in Great Britain, please contact Helion & Co. at 0121 705 3393 or
    books@helion.co.uk.

Printed in Canada

Library and Archives Canada Cataloguing in Publication

Cooke, Bert
        We're not dead yet : the First World War diary of Private Bert
Cooke / [edited by] Milly Walsh and John Callan.

(Vanwell voices of war)
Includes bibliographical references.
ISBN 1-55125-087-X

        1. Cooke, Bert. 2. World War, 1914-1918--Personal narratives,
Canadian. 3. Soldiers--Canada--Diaries. 4. Canada. Canadian Army--
Biography. I. Callan, John, 1945- II. Walsh, Milly, 1924- III. Title.
IV. Series.

D640.C66 2004   940.4'8171   C2004-903991-1

CONTENTS

In memory of Herbert Bryant Cooke

who kept a diary during the Great War

"B" Company of the 75th Battalion.

—The Cooke and Walsh families

PREFACE

This book is based on the diaries of Herbert (Bert) Cooke, who wrote a first-hand account of his experiences in France and Belgium during the First World War. The initial purpose of transcribing and editing the diaries into book format was to provide a written record for family members.

During my initial reading of the transcribed manuscript, I realized the deplorable conditions under which Bert had composed his writings, from candlelight at night to actual battle conditions. He graphically describes the daily routine and life of a foot soldier, and the realities of trench warfare.

Bert's experience was lived out by many other men like him. So, with the consent of Mrs. Walsh (Bert's niece) this book was produced so it can be shared with those readers who had relatives who fought and died in the Great War. We trust that this book may become a legacy not only to the Cooke family but also to those who made the supreme sacrifice.

Bert's diary was written solely for his own personal benefit. The true value of his writings lies in the personal perspective that it offers on the larger events.

Although Bert's diary writings have been edited for style, clarity, punctuation and grammar, every effort has been made to keep the main ideas and Bert's actual writing intact.

John Callan

ACKNOWLEDGMENTS

The authors are indebted to the following people for their efforts in confirming the spelling, existence, and name changes of the towns that Bert Cooke encountered in his travels while in France and Belgium, and for the resultant maps: Dr. Cameron Pulsifer, Historian, Canadian War Museum, Ottawa, Ontario; G.J. Bouquillon, Vice Consel, Belgian Consulate, Toronto, Ontario; Mrs. V.W. Adams and Mrs. Katrien Riem, staff, Belgian Consulate, Toronto, Ontario; Bernadette Grezes, Vice Consul, French Consulate, Toronto, Ontario; Lylianne Battiato, Information Officer, French Embassy, Ottawa, Ontario; Patrice Soulié, Redacteur en chef, Société du Bottin Administratif, Paris, France; Earl Reid, Department of History, Laurentian University, Sudbury, Ontario.

For her knowledge of family background that has resulted in the narrative, and for all the family pictures she provided, I am grateful to Mrs. Milly Walsh, Hanmer, Ontario, Bert Cooke's niece and Arthur Cooke's daughter.

George Taylor served in the 38th Battalion as a machine gunner and survived the fighting at Vimy Ridge. His son, Lloyd Taylor of Sudbury, Ontario, provided detailed information about Vimy Ridge and other battles, as well as numerous anecdotes. His information supplemented the military narrative, and confirmed the general feelings and psyche of the Canadian soldier. I thank him.

INTRODUCTION

F ew soldiers who fought in the First World War revealed the horrors they encountered. The problem for many of them was the impossibility of finding the right words to portray the indescribable.

The *indescribable* began on a Monday morning in early summer: June 29, 1914. The newspapers carried a shocking headline: Heir to Austria's Throne Slain. That item of news startled those who were alive at the time, and it set in motion a chain of events that still affects all of us today.

Behind that shocking headline lay murder, secret societies, conspiracy, jumbled alliances, racial and religious intolerance, oppression, and greed for land and power. Such was the order of the day in a mountainous area of central Europe called the Balkans.

The Balkans included Albania, Bulgaria, Greece, Romania and Yugoslavia. Yugoslavia comprised six federal republics. The largest of these was Serbia, and Bosnia, one of the smaller republics, was where, in 1914, the army of the Habsburgs chose to hold its summer manoeuvres. The Habsburgs, the ancient royal family which ruled Austria, also provided the royalty of the Balkans.

On June 25, Archduke Franz Ferdinand, nephew to Austria's Emperor Franz Josef and Inspector General of the Army, arrived in Bosnia with his wife, Sophia Chotec, Duchess of Hohenberg, to supervise the manoeuvres.

On June 28 1914, the morning after the manoeuvres concluded, the archduke drove with his wife to the provincial capital, Sarajevo. As well as official business in the capital, Ferdinand wanted to give his wife an opportunity to ride beside him in an open car on an official occasion. Franz Ferdinand had married beneath him; Sophia was not allowed, because of the rules and restrictions of his rank, to sit beside him on public occasions except when he was acting in a military capacity.

The archduke was an unpopular man among the leaders of the Austro-Hungarian Empire because of his ill-advised marriage to Sophia, and because he favoured political reform. He was proposing devolution to grant the Bosnian Slavs more liberty.

That morning, as they were being driven through the narrow streets of Sarajevo on their way to the residence of the provincial governor, a group of five young Serbians and a Bosnian Muslim, equipped with bombs and pistols, lay in wait.

The youths had been smuggled to Belgrade, the capital of Yugoslavia and Serbia, where they had received training and weapons, then smuggled back across the border with the aid of Serbian customs to carry out their cold-blooded deed. Suddenly, one of the terrorists threw a bomb at the car carrying Franz Ferdinand and his wife. The bomb didn't explode on impact. It bounced off, exploding under the car following and wounding an army officer. The imperial party sped off.

Three-quarters of an hour later, en route to visit the injured officer in hospital, Ferdinand's chauffeur took a wrong turn. While the car was in reverse, it came to a momentary halt. The stop brought the car opposite one of the undetected assassins.

The assassin was a restless, idealistic, and alienated youth of a type all too familiar in the modern world. He had failed in school. His head was filled with an intoxicating cloud of the ideas available at the end of the nineteenth century—revolution, insurgency, and resentment against the rich and powerful. Though a resident of Bosnia and technically a citizen of the Dual Monarchy (Austria-Hungary), Gavrilo Princip was a passionate Serbian patriot. He and his nineteen-year-old fellow conspirators were members of the Union of Death, or Black Hand, a secret Serbian terrorist society that received aid from the Russian government.

Gavrilo was armed with a revolver. He stepped forward out of the shadows of the narrow street, aimed, and fired. The bullet struck Sophia, killing her instantly. Princip fired again. This time the bullet struck Ferdinand. The Archduke of Austria-Hungary was dead within ten minutes. Princip was arrested on the spot.

There was every reason to suspect that the assassination was not a private act. Indeed, it was later proven that Princip and his fellow assassins were the idealistic tools of Colonel Dragutin Dimitrijevic, Chief of the Intelligence Department of the Serbian General Staff and a leading spirit in the patriotic Black Hand Society. He had planned the deed. Dimitrijevic felt that Austria-Hungary was making preparations for war against Serbia. He thought that with the disappearance of Franz Ferdinand the policies and the climate of opinion Ferdinand represented would lose its driving force, and that the danger of war would be removed.

But, significantly, Austria now had reason and opportunity to humiliate Serbia. The various diplomatic agreements entered into by Austria, Great Britain, Russia, and France were designed to protect and advance the respective political futures of each country, and action against Serbia was bound to cause a clash between the European powers.

Austria-Hungary declared war on Serbia on July 28, 1914. The Russian order of July 30 for men to enroll in the armed forces to fight for Serbia was followed by Germany's declaration of war against Russia on August 1, 1914, and against France on August 3, 1914. Germany announced to King Albert of Belgium on August 2 its intention to enter Belgium for the purpose of attacking France. Great Britain had treaty obligations to defend Belgian neutrality, so when King Albert appealed to England, Russia, and France for help in repelling the Germans, he got his help. The actions of one country affected those of another. Never had alliances been more entangling.

Germany's invasion of Belgium on August 3, 1914, forced the British Parliament's hand, and Great Britain declared war on Germany the next day. All the great powers of Europe were now at war. Germany's dreams of world domination would become the nightmare of the other European countries.

Political unity now took root inside countries. Economic control gave rise to policies and new laws geared to give total support to the war effort and the mobilization of economic resources. The regulations of economic life meant that citizens could no longer sell their labour or services as they wished, nor could they spend their wages as they would normally have done. Newspapers were subject to rigorous censorship by governments.

Amidst this backdrop of international tension and internal national turmoil, Bert Cooke and other ordinary people of that time attempted to carry on with their lives.

Herbert Bryant Cooke was born on November 16, 1880, in Bowling Green, a small suburb of Cirencester, England. Cirencester was a wool-marketing town located on the banks of the Churn River in the urban district of Gloucestershire 153 kilometres (95 miles) northwest of London.

Bert was the son of James Cooke, who had been born in 1853 in Queensford, Calne, in the county of Wiltshire, west of London. In his adult life James became a minister and a butcher. Bert's mother, Delila Ann Walton, was native to the Cirencester area. Shortly after James came to Cirencester he married Delila, and they set up their home there. Delila Cooke owned a hand-laundry business that she continued even during the years of the war. James and Delila had a family of ten: four girls and six boys. Bert was the oldest brother, followed by Walter, Fred, the twins, Ralph and Arthur, and Sidney.

Bert left school at the age of ten to work as a ploughboy on farms in the countryside surrounding Cirencester. Leaving school at an early age did not discourage his thirst for knowledge. His spare time was spent reading magazines, mostly of a geographical nature, to feed his intelligent, inquisitive mind. In his teen years Bert served three years with the Somerset Light Infantry, a military experience that mentally prepared him to tolerate the constant drill that would plague recruits during the war years.

Bert, along with his brother Arthur, also worked in their father's butcher shop in Cirencester, but Bert dreamed of owning his own butcher shop. Near his father's butcher shop was a shoe repair shop. Every time Bert took the family's shoes for repair he stayed on, watching intently as the cobbler worked. Inevitably, Bert gained a working knowledge of the trade from the shop owner.

Growing up, all the boys belonged to some type of band, and each of the boys performed with his respective band at different social gatherings about once a week. Other than playing in a band, golfing, wrestling, and boxing kept Bert entertained. It is not hard to imagine that his voracious appetite ignited an interest in cooking. He loved to cook. Bert's love of food and eating became a bit of a curse to him as a soldier of the "Jolly 75th."

All the boys knew what work was about at an early age. They were all tall, stout, strong, strapping lads, none less than six feet tall, who helped support the family financially. Bert was not only strong physically, but he also had an extremely strong will, tempered with a sense of humour. Endurance and determination completed his character. These inherent qualities eventually helped him endure one of the worst clashes the world would ever experience.

In 1905, at the age of twenty-five, Bert married twenty-six-year-old Auguster "Gus" Hollings, a native of Cirencester. Bert and Auguster had two sons, Morris and Harold. After the birth of his second son Harold in May of 1910, life for Bert and his family followed a pleasant routine. The weekdays were taken up with work and the regular activities required in raising a family. While Bert worked in his father's butcher shop, Auguster helped out with the hand-laundry business that Bert's mother Delila owned. The real quality time with Gus and the boys came on the weekends. Bert read to his boys, and his imagination made him a great storyteller too.

Bert's dream of having his own business was still strong, and in 1913, he bought passage on an Irish steamer, the RMS *Araguaya*, and went to Canada with his brother Arthur. Bert thought that Canada afforded more opportunity for pursuing his business goals. He established a small delicatessen on Danforth Avenue in Toronto, Ontario. After acquiring a home on Church Street near his Danforth Avenue delicatessen, he sent for Auguster and the boys.

By the time the war erupted, four of Bert's brothers had enlisted. Fred and Walter had joined the British army, and Ralph had enlisted with the 5th Field Ambulance Corps of the Royal Canadian Army on November 24, 1914. In November 1915, Bert learned that Arthur was planning to join the 87th Grenadier Guards of the Canadian army. Sidney had also signed up with the British army by this time. So, after much contemplation, Bert decided it was time for him to follow in the footsteps of his brothers. On November 23, 1915, Bert enlisted in the 75th Canadian Battalion.

Auguster remained in Canada during the early part of Bert's tour of duty, and supported herself and her sons by opening up a hat shop business. As the war dragged on, however, she and the boys decided to go back to England to be closer to Bert. The delicatessen Bert had established was sold.

Bert returned to Toronto with his family after the war, and resumed his business in the butcher trade by opening another delicatessen on Danforth Avenue, this time with his eldest son Morris. Auguster had saved up money from her hat shop so that Bert would be able to follow this path after the war.

At the age of thirty, Morris moved to Vancouver, British Columbia, where he opened his own delicatessen. After Morris left the butcher shop, Bert and his youngest son Harold continued managing it for many years. Harold took over when his father retired.

Bert's brother Arthur also returned to Canada after the war and lived in Hudson, Quebec. He became a greens keeper and golf course designer at the Hudson Golf Course. Arthur married twice. He had three children with his first wife, and five boys and one girl with his second.

In the years after the war Arthur developed a tumor in his esophagus, a direct result of being gassed during the war. He died before he reached fifty-five, after an operation on the tumor.

Arthur's twin, Ralph, came to Canada in the 1920s and worked for the Canadian Pacific Railway. He did marry and died two years after Arthur.

Walter became a military policeman in the British army after the war and rose to the rank of corporal. He married and had a family of two boys and two girls. Walter lived his remaining years in England.

Fred reached the rank of sergeant during his military service. Like Walter, he lived his remaining years in England.

Sidney, the youngest of Bert's brothers, had two daughters, one of whom was killed during a German bombing raid on London. Sidney lived his remaining years in England after serving with Lord Kitchener's army during the war, and died a few years after Arthur.

In the early part of 1926, upon Arthur's suggestion, James and Delila relocated to the Beaches area of Toronto to be close to their children.

In December of 1932, Bert's mother Delila died at the age of seventy-four. Three years later James Cooke died at the age of eighty-two.

Bert's wife Auguster died at the age of seventy-four, and five years later, in August 1958, Bert Cooke joined his wife and parents in the family plot at St. James Cemetery in Toronto, Ontario.

After Bert died, his son Harold took possession of his father's diaries, poems, and the letters Bert had written while in the army. In 1990, Harold gave the diaries to his cousin Milly Walsh. Until that time Mrs. Walsh had had no idea that the diaries ever existed.

What compelled a young man who had never kept any type of childhood journal to chronicle his life during the First World War? Bert probably understood that he was undergoing the experience of a lifetime and wanted to leave a memoir of the Great War for his family.

Bert's diary chronicles what he witnessed, experienced himself, or had told to him by fellow soldiers and the people he met personally. It is Bert's story of his part in the war. He had no other ambition than to record as faithfully as he could, the events in which he took part. Bert displayed no bitterness about his war experience as a whole. He accepted the responsibility that came with being a soldier, did his duty, and was happy to get back to civilian life, even though his tour of duty was longer than he expected. Bert's diary was eloquently written only to provide a written record for the immediate family, to tell them and their descendants how one of their own had fared in those turbulent times.

Two of Bert's actual diaries. (Peter Hubbard)

The family of James and Delila Cooke. Back row, left to right: Bert, Ralph, Arthur, Walter, Florence, and James. Front row: Gus (holding Morris), Eva, James, Sidney (seated), Bertha, and Delila (holding Norah).
(Milly Walsh)

Bert's parents, James and Delila Cooke. (Milly Walsh)

The Bert Cooke family, left to right: Bert, his son, Harold, his wife, Auguster Hallings Cooke, and son Morris. (Milly Walsh)

Bert Cooke standing behind the counter of his butcher shop.
(Milly Walsh)

Bert Cooke (left) standing outside his butcher shop with his brother, Arthur Cooke. (Milly Walsh)

The Cooke family coat of arms. (Milly Walsh)

CHAPTER 1

Training A New Recruit

One poor fellow with a wife and six children by her side made me wonder why a person in such a situation would want to join the army, perhaps never to see his family again. Nevertheless, it showed the spirit of the Canadians.

Passage from Bert Cooke's diary

Deep in his heart Bert Cooke's religious upbringing told him that the war was morally wrong. Within two years his view of the Germans would drastically change. His moral values and sense of fair play had been challenged by, as he put it, "their doggish tricks sinking ships with poor women and children aboard without the slightest warning."

Bert was a man of his word with strong convictions. Now he was ready to back up his convictions and ideology with positive action, so Bert followed in the footsteps of his brothers, feeling compelled to "do his bit." Despite the physical and emotional ordeal he knew lay before him, Bert joined the 75th Canadian Battalion on November 23, 1915, at the age of thirty-five. Bert became Private Bert Cooke, a rank that he kept throughout his military service.

Little did I think when we were young, and all things around us were gay, that some fine day our monarch would say, it's up to every person to do his duty. After living for so many years in peace and happiness, it was cruel for such a war between so many countries to start. Little did we think that it would mean the calling of so many human beings together to be slaughtered like sheep for the sake of a few individuals who thought they could conquer the world. Alas, they did not consider the individuals in the Colonies who were willing to aid the motherland. These individuals were willing to lay down their lives for the honourable old flag that had protected us so long.

For instance, take Canada. Some people said this is not a war for us. The mass of the Canadian people had hardly come to think in terms of war at all! But I must tell you, before the war was many days old, the Canadian government promptly called England offering the service of Canadian troops. The offer was accepted with gratitude.

Now the call came for individuals to fight for their country. Did they say, "No, fight your own battle. This is nothing to do with us." No! Individuals flocked to the colours and were proud to do their bit for King and Country. Over 300,000 human beings joined the Canadian army and would die to save their flag from being crushed under by those cursed Huns. I must say that the boys have done well. They have proved to be individuals in this terrible struggle. They will fight to the embittered end.

Now I will tell you a little about my experience as a soldier and how and why I joined the army to do my bit.

At the commencement of the war, it was my ambition to become a soldier. Then, it was impossible for me to do so or even think of such a thing, although my heart was in the right place.

I had to forgo enlisting after a few weeks. I heard from England that my brother Walter, had served his time in the "King's Life Guards" before the war. He was now transferred to France. There he had varied experiences and some very close calls several times. He had also won himself the "Russian Cross of St. George," being decorated by Nicholas II, the Czar of Russia. After another short period, I received another letter saying that another brother, Fred, had joined Lord Kitchener's Army. He was transferred shortly after to Salonika.

By this time I was feeling very uncomfortable.

My third brother, Arthur, who was staying with me in Canada, had enlisted and Ralph, twin brother to Arthur, also joined the Fifth Field Ambulance Corps to go on overseas. Their enlistments eased my mind for a time. Then news came again from England. My youngest brother Sidney had joined Lord Kitchener's Army too, so I began thinking whether the time was right for me to do something.

After waiting a few days, the opportunity came for me to become a soldier. I made up my mind to go down to the armory and join. Pausing briefly at the door, I went in and passed the doctors' test. The day was November 23, 1915.

It was rather difficult for me to select a Battalion. But I decided after careful consideration to join the Old Toronto Corps known as the Mississauga Horse, now called the 75th Battalion.

The evening of November 25 was the most memorable when we were staying at the Barracks of the 75th. The boys all sang and gave us recruits such a welcome that it would be hard to forget.

The next thing was to be assigned to a Company. I was assigned to "B" Company 6th Platoon. After being introduced to the men, I had to find a place to sleep. It was a wooden bunk, just a place for one on the top and the other below. I discovered the top bunk was the best one after a little more experience.

Sleeping was almost impossible as the boards were hard. Nevertheless, it was time to start the day. We had roll call followed by a wash. The time came for the thing I was waiting for, breakfast! I ate very little because it was different to the breakfasts I usually ate. You can picture me sitting down and gazing at the food before me.

The next thing on the program was to obtain my full issue of clothes. It was amusing trying to get things to fit me. Some of my clothing was two inches too small, while others were about six inches too big. So you see, it took quite a few days for me to get fully equipped. Notwithstanding all this, I had heard a little about how to become an efficient soldier. Being an efficient soldier meant that I had to begin drill.

At first, it did not seem hard to me as I had served in the volunteers [Somerset Light Infantry] in England when I was quite a young fellow, but things had changed. It was hard work to get fit for the trenches, but I was ready to do what ever was necessary. Just then, when I was about a week there, I learned that my fifth brother living in Montreal had also joined. For a family of six boys this is not a shabby record.

I settled down to the soldier's life, although it was a tough proposition for me. I had had the best of everything and was always my own boss. Now I had many [bosses]. I must say that I got along very well with the officers and always obeyed orders.

The worst had yet to come. The winter was beginning, and it was no easy task to drill in about two or three feet of snow. The weather was below zero, but it didn't kill me. At times I felt like dropping out after a long route march with full pack. I often used to say that a soldier was a thing to hang a load on, and a heavy load it was! But, I became used to it and soon relaxed. You must remember the other men had seen about four months training at Niagara. They marched from Niagara to the winter quarters in Toronto, a distance of about one hundred miles without even losing one man. So you see, I had well-seasoned men to train alongside. I pulled through after serving about two months in the lines.

A call came for a shoemaker to help repair boots for the recruits. Having knowledge of the trade, I decided to try to get in the repair shop and help. I was successful and started on my new work, January 15, 1916. At least we could work to keep ourselves warm. I found that better than tramping down snow and nearly freezing.

Going over to England was the next thing we were thinking. Every day brought a rumor that we would be moving in a day or so. We got sick of listening to the tales of when we had to go overseas. The time did come, and arrangements were made for us to proceed to England on April 5, 1916. They gave one half of the battalion four days leave to say good-bye to their friends.

It came my time for leave going with the second half of the battalion. Alas, before we had been gone one day, the commander ordered our return. Orders stated we were to start a week earlier than the date mentioned. Canceling our leave did not upset us as we were all eager to get over to England.

The date for us to leave was March 28, 1916, which was a Sunday. Never in my life shall I forget that day. All the wives, sweethearts, and friends were summoned into our quarters. Between men, women and children, the place was packed from two o'clock that afternoon until eight-thirty in the evening. When the bugle sounded fall-in, we buckled on our kits. I thought I could stand almost anything. But, that night found a soft spot in my heart for some of the mothers and wives of those boys. One poor fellow with a wife and six children by her side made me wonder why a person in such a situation would want to join the army, perhaps never to see his family again. Nevertheless, it showed the spirit of the Canadians.

We had to march into a huge building to allow the people to go to their homes. For nearly three hours we stood loading up, ready to march off to the train, which was waiting for us near our quarters. After all our waiting, crowds of people stood to cheer us on as we had orders to entrain. The band struck up the "Maple Leaf" and off we marched to the train through water and mud.

After a struggle, we reached the train, relieved to unload our packs and get seated. After that, the news came for us to settle down and get some sleep as we would not pull out until morning. I can tell you it was much-needed sleep.

The train we occupied had bunks for sleeping. But since we had a three-day ride, we had to make ourselves comfortable for the journey. About two o'clock in the morning we pulled out of the station and continued on our journey. To our surprise people were watchful all along the line to wish us God speed and a safe return.

After getting away from Toronto, we settled down for a much-needed rest after the excitement we had experienced. Although our sleeping compartments were uncomfortable, I managed to sleep a few hours. When I awoke, we were well on our way to Halifax.

The next thing to think about was breakfast, and it was pandemonium to see the persons carrying rations for the men up and down the train. Sometimes it was worse than being on a ship as the coach seemed to rock backwards and forwards, and then you would see everything falling all around us. It was most amusing.

After breakfast was cleared we could do as we pleased. We could read, play cards or do anything we liked except get off the train. Guards stationed at each door ensured that no person left the train. It was like being in prison. Dinner followed later in the same manner. Then, it was sleep or do anything we wanted. Many of the men wrote letters and dropped them off at the different stations or with any person who would post them.

The first day on the train was pleasant, but the second day became tiresome. A walk in the fresh air would have done us good. So, they arranged to stop at a certain town and let us out for a walk.

Eventually we arrived at the town where we experienced a march. It felt strange to walk around after being penned up like cattle. But, we formed up and started off for about twenty-five minutes. The people gave us a hearty welcome without a cheer. They gazed at us as though we were escapees. I suppose it was because of the people being French Canadians. They are not so enthusiastic as the English people, but we did not mind that. It was the fresh air and exercise that we needed.

Herded on to the train, off we went again, this being the second time on the train. We were fed up with the journey, but the night came, and it was time to curl up and go to sleep. Sometimes you would be tossed around as the train continued to roll along.

Morning came on the third day and the breakfast served consisted only of sausages. I remember well the man who was serving them fell. As he was falling, the "poor, old mystery bags" dropped, scattering on the floor as if delighted to be released. All the same, they were devoured by the men that did not see the accident.

Another walk was arranged to let us out again. The town band was there to receive us and there were crowds of people to welcome us. They had cheers and hand shakes; all the women were raving to get our badges or some little item as a keepsake. I must say it was pleasant, despite marching through all the mud and slush.

It was refreshing to get a stretch after our march.

We were hustled back to the train once more. Off we went again, but in a short time we came to a stand still on a curve in the railway track. It was impossible for the large engine to move. So, it became necessary to return to the town we had just passed through to get another engine. After an hour we pushed off again. By that time it was nearly the hour to sleep. After a little walk we bedded ourselves down for the night. This being the last night on the train, we made the best of it and had a good time.

We arrived at Halifax about three in the morning, and glad we were here. By that time we felt like a lot of old men. The time had come for our last breakfast on the train that consisted of sausage, tea, and bread. The good old sausage was always a standby. After we had partaken of the hearty breakfast, we had orders to pack up and buckle our harness and make a move to the docks. The whole time we were kept in the dark as to which ship we were taking.

Prime Minister Sir Robert Borden initially had expected Canada's overseas man-power needs would be met voluntarily, but enlistments had begun to thin out by the middle of 1915. All the units reached full strength, but in some cases recruiting to full strength was a struggle. A recruiting campaign, it was found, cost money. To get recruits, it became necessary for the government to appeal for them, in the press, on the platform and in the street. Posters were pasted on store-fronts and walls, and flyers were distributed by hand. It became necessary for battalions to solicit financial support from the public. Following the outbreak of the war, militia units across Canada acted as recruiting stations.

It was at this juncture that the demand was first heard for compulsory military service, or conscription. In the opinion of the government, however, the country was not yet ripe for conscription, so the militia department kept on trying to secure recruits through voluntary service.

Those who were coming forward were married men with families, whereas many unmarried men were holding back from enlisting. This was certain to cost the country heavily in separation allowances, patriotic fund grants and pensions. From the standpoint of finance, it was contended that a system of recruiting that created such a condition of affairs was wrong. So it was urged that the state indicate who should go. By the end of 1915, recruitment had declined so much that Ottawa allowed patriotic-minded groups of citizens to raise units at their own expense.

In January 1916, Borden announced a Canadian overseas commitment of 500,000 men, an almost unsustainable number of voluntary enlistments from a population of barely eight million. In August 1917 the government passed the Military Act imposing conscription. French Canada bitterly opposed the measure, as did farmers and labour groups. Canadians became deeply divided over the issue.

Earl Horatio Herbert, Kitchener.
(The John A. Hertel Co. Ltd., Toronto, 1919)

Left to right: Ralph, Arthur, and Bert Cooke. (Milly Walsh)

The shoe shop. (Milly Walsh)

CHAPTER 2

The Voyage

The excitement of the journey was mounting as we were thinking of the sub-marines that were prowling the sea for prey.

Passage from Bert Cooke's diary

Bert wrote the following letter to his wife Auguster during his voyage to Europe:

139245
Mr. H.B. Cooke
B. Company
75th Battalion
On Board HMS Troop Ship
Empress of Britain

On the last Sunday night of March 1916, we entrained for Halifax. It was a night of all nights for the 75th. All day until the word came to fall-in, it was joy in all parts of the barracks. But when the bugle sounded fall-in, there were wives clinging to their husbands, mothers their sons, and sweethearts to their loved ones. A sight never to be forgotten by all. About two hours after being called up, through the cheering to board the train as our band played "Auld Lang Syne." It was a heavy march as the mud was so thick. We finally reached the train and boarded her, and I can assure you it was a relief to take our packs off.

The next thing to do was to get fixed up for our journey to the coast on the train which was long and weary. After getting fixed up, we were told to get down to sleep as we would not pull out until the morning. So, we made ourselves comfortable and went to sleep and woke up to find ourselves on our way. The next thing to think of was breakfast. After a lot of fuss we were served a slice of bread with a little butter painted on with a paintbrush and two sausages, a little dish of porridge and coffee. After breakfast, roll call to see if any of the men had escaped, but all were present. After a few hours it was time to think of a dinner of stew and bread pudding and a little tea. It made our mouths water to see the waiters taking the food to the officers' mess. Of course, they must have their fancy dishes, or I think they would die. After dinner we would sit around and smoke or play cards. Anything to wear away the time. Then tea with cheese, jam and bread. After tea it was a little singing and a few jokes and then bed.

After being on the train for two days and three nights we arrived at Halifax. Along the way we had to get off the train at two towns and had a march around the town. At one place the town band met us as we arrived. The street was lined with people to cheer us on our way. After our train journey we had to load ourselves again to proceed to the ship. To our surprise the Mayor of Toronto had traveled with us to see the regiment off. As he called for us to embark, he wished us all the luck and a safe return. We marched to the docks and found the *Empress of Britain* waiting for us. We were all aboard, then came the 74th Battalion. Also, from Toronto a West of Canada Battalion, after that came the Army Medical Corp. Then came a draft of Artillery. It was remarkable. We all wondered where they could put us all, but we were all quartered. I can tell you it isn't all honey on a troop ship. We were on the third deck. Down there were twenty-four of us at one table and no room to turn. Every man has his place—packed like cattle.

When we finally got fixed up, we wandered around until we got on the main deck and watched the other soldiers come aboard. Dinnertime came but no dinner was served, and I can assure you I was mighty hungry as we had breakfast on the train at 5:00 a.m. We had to wait until the tea was served, but the excitement seemed to fill us, as every soldier was anxious to get aboard. Tea was served about 5:00 p.m. Tea consisted of a small loaf of bread and butter with jam. The next thing to think about was how we were going to sleep as there were no beds to sleep in. But we discovered that there were hooks above our heads, and we found that we had to sleep in hammocks swinging up to the ceiling. Then, the fun started as the light is limited. When you come down at first, you can hardly see. But we managed to find our beds, and it was a sight to see the men fixing up, and getting into these hammocks.

Some of the men couldn't sleep in them but had to take them up on the upper decks and sleep on the floor. We got through that night. The next thing was to get men off for breakfast, and I can tell you it was like a circus to see these men waiting at the cookhouse. It is a big thing to feed and keep four thousand soldiers. After waiting about two hours, we got our breakfast and to our surprise it was sausage again. They fed us on the train with sausages and then sausages on the ship. I wonder if they will feed us the old sausage in England. We had a little loaf of bread and butter and tea. What I look forward to is the little loaf of bread and butter, as it's very good.

After breakfast we went up on deck, and then we wondered when we were going to sail. But we were told that three boats had to be loaded up before we could sail as they were going to escort us over with gunboats. We pulled out of dock on Thursday at 3:00 p.m., only to anchor in the harbour until the other ships were loaded. We settled down to wonder when we were going to sail but it came at last. We set off in a fog about midday, Saturday, April 1, every soldier, about four thousand beside the crew of the ship, lined the decks and other boats lying in dock had their men out to cheer us on our way. It was a grand sight to see a battalion ship leading three troop ships with over ten thousand soldiers aboard steaming out of port. The fog got so thick we lost sight of the other ships, and they had to keep blowing their whistles, starting with the battalion ship, then the others in order, just to know that they were all in order. Our ship being the fastest one had to keep in the rear.

Sometimes we had to pull up as we were too near the other ships. It was difficult in the fog to tell how far we were behind. The fog lasted for two days, and on the third day the sky was clear and the weather fine.

Now a little about the boys, how they are faring on the ship. It is most amusing to see them at night looking for a place to sleep. They start carrying their blankets and getting into the lifeboats or in amongst the ropes or any place rather than sleep down below. It is amazing to think that we eat on the table and sleep on the ceiling over the table. The odour is terrible, especially in the morning when they get up for breakfast. The night is the dullest time of all. There are no lights on deck, and no man is allowed to smoke. All you can do is get to bed. The men play cards and gamble till 9:00 p.m., then you hear the men who didn't fix up their beds start roaring. They are also forbidden to smoke or light a match. But sometimes you will see someone that has no respect for himself or any other person light a match. Then you hear a roar: "Put that light out." If it was to catch on fire, we would not have a ghost of a chance to get out.

Every day at 10:00 a.m. we have a parade with lifebelts on as there is one for every man, and all the soldiers have to line up on the deck. The Captain of the ship with the head of the different regiments inspects them—they inspect the ship as there are soldiers who are told off every day to clean the quarters. Two men each day are told to look after one table of twenty-four men. They have to fetch the food and serve it out and wash the dishes and keep the place clean. Every man has to take his turn. It's fun to watch the men waiting to get the food, they line up at the cookhouse about two hours before you can get served. It makes a fellow sick waiting so long, and then you have to be careful how it is served up or some will have to go short, as there are always fellows looking for more than their share. The first day it was difficult for every man to get enough to eat as the sea air gave them such an appetite. They could eat twice as much, but the second day we found some of them missing. All you had to do was go into the lavatory or on deck rails and see them bringing up all they had eaten on the trip and wishing they had stayed at home or for the ship to sink. It was awful to see their faces. The third day was worse—there was lots of food for all and lots left. The boys were lying all around—they wouldn't venture upon the deck—there they lay in the passages or any place where they could not feel the motion of the ship. It was painful to see them.

Today the fog lifted and I was an early riser this morning as I had pains in my stomach after taking a few pills the night before which caused me to walk over the sleeping men on the floor and on the ceiling to get to a place where I could ease myself. I can tell you, it is misery when you arrive at the place to see a line-up waiting their turn with awful-looking faces—it is painful. The convenience on the ship for so many men is absolutely rotten, it is all right to get so many men on the ship as possible but it's bad for the men. I can tell you, if the men had known what they would have to put up with, they never would have boarded the ship. Every day there has to be so many men on guard and on special duty. Every man has to go a special way to his own quarters and sometimes you have to go from one side of the ship to the other to get down to your quarters.

It makes a fellow mad sometimes, especially when you find the officers have such fine times and everything for their comfort. It is a pleasure trip for them but agony for lots of the men. Another thing I haven't mentioned is the way which the stokers and crew on ship sell things to the boys. They make lemonade and charge ten cents a glass and tea and all that kind of thing charging three times the price it is worth.

They think we have lots of money to spend, and are out to get it if a man is foolish enough to buy from them.

Seeing I am one of the men to get the food today, I will have to put my writing away. We have just cleaned breakfast away and we will soon have to line up for dinner. It takes such a long time to get the food— one man gives you butter, which is margarine. Then you have to go to another place for bread, then you have to go to another place for meat, then another place for tea or coffee. After you have made that trip and arrive at your table, it makes a fellow feel as though he doesn't want any food. I am now going up on deck to get a little fresh air before I parade for dinner.

After another day of travelling I sit down and write a few more lines about my experience on the ship. There is a certain class of men on board that certainly are enjoying this trip, and that is the men that run what they call a gambling school. Some of them have made a lot of money, others have lost all they had and are only too pleased to do what are called mess orderlies for the rest of the journey to earn a little money to have when they reach England. Another thing that caused quite a controversy was the men getting allowances of beer per day. Other troops carried by this ship were allowed one pint a day and our officers were taking their liquor, so the Captain of the ship had a little talk with the officers about the men having their share. But the officers thought the men shouldn't have any. Well, said the Captain, if the men can't have their drinks by your permission you can't have yours. He made it a dry ship which I thought was very good of him; that is British fair play.

Now we are getting more used to things and some of the boys are having the time of their lives. It seems to be like a large family. Never before since the battalion was formed have the boys been so attached to each other. They play and joke as never before. I have seen men in the barracks and if you said a word to them they would get mad, but now they take everything in good part. Another thing you can see is that the men that were always drinking are sensible for the first time. They look better and feel better in every respect. We are having a very smooth trip. The boys are just getting over the seasickness. There are quite a few that still remain on deck and have to be fed. It isn't a joke to see a man sick and unable to eat. Just take a nice piece of fat meat and show it to him, he will make for you at once.

Another bit of fun is when we are having a little exercise in the morning. The boat does a little roll then we all roll in a heap on deck. As you can see over four thousand soldiers trying to drill on a ship, it's just a joke and we all act like schoolboys.

Another little experience I have had, some of the men who are not used to shaving themselves on ships—me having a steady hand, I have this chance to be barber to them. I am able to shave them as good as a barber—it was a little nerve-wracking at first, but now I can sweep around them all right. Between being carver at the table I am also of men's faces.

Taking up food to the sick pals and one thing and another, I am a pretty busy man. It wears away the time, and it also amuses me. Today we have an armed guard. Nearly a hundred soldiers with loaded rifles at each end of the ship. Now we are getting into the danger zone. We also have a large gun at the rear end of the ship, which is operated by old navy men. We also have our machine guns set along the deck and it is nice to see the warships guarding us. It will go at full speed and get in front of the three ships, then pull up and get level with the last ship. We have a good view watching it. I am nearly at the end of my paper and I think I have nearly said all, but I will try and give you a few more words in my next edition. We had some nice prunes for dessert today, but they had a lot of maggots in them. It was not a very nice finish for the boys that expected to keep their dinner down.

I will leave you to guess the rest. Well, I will close my few words in saying that the sooner this journey is over the better I shall be pleased. I tried to sleep on deck last night, but it was so cold I had to go down below and hang myself upon the ceiling in the warmth. Well, I will close with these few words.

Bert

Perhaps wishing to spare Auguster the grimmer details of shipboard life, Bert saved them for his diary. Auguster got the edited version, though the mention of the maggoty prunes must have given her a hint of the trials Bert—and all the enlisted men—faced on board the Empress of Britain. These were many, as we see from his diary entries about the voyage.

When we reached the dock, we could see for ourselves it was the *Empress of Britain* waiting to receive us. The boys of the 75th were the first to embark. When we got aboard the ship, we wondered after going down from one deck to the other, how much farther down we had to go. Finally, we came to our quarters, and we were very glad to lighten ourselves of the packs we were carrying. I looked around and wondered where the Sam hell we could sleep. After looking around carefully, I discovered that we had to sleep by the ceiling just above our tables where we had our food. It was a joke to get a sleeping place.

We went up to the main deck to watch the other troops board the ship. This happened after getting fitted-up and places selected to suit ourselves. Four Battalions were to come aboard as well as ammunitions, provisions, and coal for the journey. It took all that day and night and half the next to load the ship. We were all eager to know when she was going to pull out of the harbour.

I must go back and tell you about the first night on the ship. It was a rush for the hammocks because we had to sleep in them. We had to string them up to the ceiling on hooks that were screwed into the beams of the ship. Some of the men used strange language as they had their beds on the wrong hooks. After much excitement, we managed to be fixed up. We really needed a fan to cool us rather than two blankets to keep us warm. Fancy about five hundred men in a room, with very little but foul air hanging from the ceiling. It was neither pleasant nor healthy, but we had to stick it out.

The next thing was to get up in the morning, dress and pack away your hammock and hide it if you wanted to keep the same one. Being rather particular, I was eager to keep mine. So, I found a safe place to store my bed for the time I slept on the ship.

The next step was breakfast. Twenty-four men were assigned to a table. Two men were pulled off every day for what the officers called mess orderlies. They had to draw the food, serve the men and wash the dishes. With four thousand men on the ship and only one kitchen to serve from, you can imagine the time required to serve them; but they had a competent system. These two men from each table had to take turns as orderlies, sometimes having to wait about two hours before being served themselves. They always carried their tins with them. They had to gauge the time as we always sat down at the same time for our food. You would wonder sometimes how twenty-four men were going to get enough to eat. For the first two days there did not seem to be enough food. But, when we pulled out to sea, plenty of food was provided and some to spare.

The second day on the ship still found us docked. The entire group was eager to pull out. About noon that day, we were towed out into the harbour only to anchor out of sight and make believe we had sailed. No person could see us there. Thick fog surrounded us all night.

In the morning after the fog lifted, we became excited and began to wonder when we were going to leave for England. The time came around noon, and we started with two other transports loaded with troops, and ready to continue with us. We did pull out in fog.

After leaving the harbour, we could see very little, but we knew England was our destination. Also, a warship was escorting us. Owing to the submarine scare it was necessary to have an additional escort.

So, several other men plus myself wanted to be on deck for a while to watch for anything exciting. Several of us nearly forgot supper.

The motion of the ship began to tell on some of the boys who had not crossed the ocean before. It made me feel good, and I just went below doing justice to a plain supper. The fun did start that night because our quarters were near the boilers and the heat was terrible especially when all the boys were ordered down. We got our little cots set up. But it was too hot to sleep because all the portholes had to be closed, and all lights extinguished.

You can imagine what it was like. We called it a death trap, but at the same time we had our fun. One man would start pushing then the whole row would be rocking, and others would turn over and fall upon the table. Those boys would shout all kinds of comical things to you. Another thing, we were not allowed to strike a match down there, but you would be surprised that most of those men would light up their cigarettes and smoke nearly all night. Then, you would hear a shout, "Put out that light!" Then, you would get your answer.

We managed to survive that night but I had made up my mind to find a healthier spot to sleep for the rest of voyage. By that time the ship had the nasty habit of rocking to and fro and hurling from side to side. Consequently, the boys were beginning to feel a queasy sensation. That night I had no sleep. When I managed a few winks, I dreamed that I was at a picnic party riding on a rig filled with strawberries. I was having the time of my life.

Many of the fellows were feeding fish with scraps of food eaten the day before. Several of the fellows were apprehensive about walking up stairs to get fresh air. They would lie around in a corner and try to forget they were living like this. You had to say to them, "How would you like a fat piece of pork for breakfast?" or something like that. Believe me you would have to run! It was amusing to me as I felt good and made it my business to help the boys as much as possible. I would help others up stairs and get them out into the air. That created the problem of how to get them back down those stairs.

Sometimes I would be asked to shave a man. Shaving is no easy matter especially when the boat is rolling, but I managed to do the job.

Some of us decided to get our beds and take them up on the top deck to sleep. My pal and I slept side by side, and it was like being in heaven after the place below. Then, we saw the fun. For the remainder of the trip, every person who could find a place to lay his blanket down was up on the deck too.

When you had supper, you had to pick up your bed and get to your place and secure it, or you would lose it. Well, that was all right. By this time many of the boys were feeling sick, too sick to parade in the morning and for a little drill and inspection.

The most amusing part about the whole trip was that sometimes it was well nigh impossible to get a wash. You would have to line up like going to a show. It was first come first serve. Perhaps, by the time your turn came the water would be shut off. Then, you would hear a few choice words uttered.

It was one big fiasco, and we were the actors. Sometimes I would think, well, I will get down to the wash house early in the morning. You would discover instead, men sprawled all along the passages, in the wash-house and in every corner. The men would sleep anywhere to get away from the "refreshing" smell of the lower decks, and other discomforts. You could cut the atmosphere with a knife!

Perhaps, you might say, "Why not open the portholes and let the fresh air in?" but our compartments were too near the water line. Had we opened the windows our beautiful furnished rooms would have been spoiled by the water gushing in.

We did take a chance one day when we were all seated and enjoying the splendid meal that was before us. As the ship rolled, a wave disturbed us causing a few of us to change our underwear. The language was charged, and the windows closed. By this time we were all on our way across the ocean.

The excitement of the journey was mounting as we were thinking of the submarines that were prowling the sea for prey.

An escort appeared on the scene within a few miles of the danger zone. Six torpedo boats were with a massive cruiser. The cruiser was leading seven war ships and five troop ships. It was like a hen with her chickens, to see these torpedo boats escorting us across the ocean. They popped in and out between us. It was amusing to sit on deck and watch the operation. It would have been an enormous victory for those Germans to get us.

We had quite a bit of sports. I wrestled with several men and came out a winner, but falling on the deck was hard. The rolling of the ship would not allow boxing.

When we paraded every morning at 10:00 a.m., we had lots of sport knocking each other around.

The Captain has stopped the gambling. He should have done that in the first place because a lot of men became penniless.

Life was getting stale, and we were all eager to get our feet on the ground again. I didn't care for the submarine scare. All day long men would hang on to their life belts for dear life.

We were nearing the end of our trip. In fact, it was the last night aboard. Every man who could find a place to sleep on the main deck was there. After getting nicely settled, a commotion erupted in the water not far away. I happened to be awake and saw our little torpedo boats dart to a certain spot. At once, flash signals from the Captain operated in zigzag fashion.

We were eager to see land, and it came at last. All eyes were gazing on the coast of Ireland. Not knowing where we would land was the best part.

The following letter to Auguster was started while Bert was still on the ship but wasn't completed until after he and the battalion had reached Bramshott camp.

My Dearest,

After a few more days of experience on a troop ship, I sit down to write a few more lines. Since writing the other news, the ship has taken another change. She is doing all kinds of stunts to get the boys going. This time she is rolling from one side to the other, and the boys that haven't had any ocean traveling before are awfully upset. They say all kinds of things and think she will turn right over. When I was asleep on deck the other night, or trying to sleep, she rolled so badly that sometimes I was on my feet. The next minute I was on my head. I can assure you I had no sleep that night at all. When I did take a few winks I dreamed I was on a picnic party riding on a rig filled with strawberries and having the time of my life, while lots of the fellows were feeding the fish with food they had eaten the day before.

The next day being in the danger zone all these poor fellows were submarine sick. All they do is to walk about with their life belts on and waiting for a crash, but they were greatly relieved when they saw we had about seven warships around us in and out and all around the three troop ships. It is funny where they all come from in a few minutes. But it was great relief for the soldiers. It is like watching a hen with her chickens to see these torpedo boats escorting us across the ocean.

We are now near Ireland and it's beautiful weather. The sun is hot and the men lie around on the deck like sheep, and we are having quite a bit of sports. I wrestled with quite a few of the fellows and came out victorious, but the deck was rather hard to fall on. We didn't have any boxing because the rolling of the ship wouldn't allow it. When we parade every morning at 10:00 a.m. we have a lot of fun knocking each other around. There is another thing that has happened. The Captain has stopped all gambling, but they should have done that in the first place as a lot of soldiers are absolutely penniless. Another funny thing, some of the boys think we will never get to England as they say we must be going around in a circle. I am just waiting for my, what they call supper. It is rotten and the tea? Well, I can tell you, I am longing for a good cup of tea and a good feed. It is awful after being used to something better, but we must be content for a while. It makes us feel as though we haven't been thankful enough for our food in the past, but believe me it will make men appreciate their home table when they get home once again.

I will tell you a little more after waiting a day. This is our last night at sea, and it was the experience of the voyage. Nearly all the men slept on deck as they were afraid of the chances of being sunk. This was Saturday night, and we all rushed to the deck nearly all in a heap to sleep. We slept until about 8:30 p.m. Some of us woke and saw the signal from our torpedo boats that there were enemy submarines all around us—in a minute we saw the warship shoot off like a dart. Then a submarine was sighted just about to sink us, but they dashed for it as she was about to strike us. They managed to capture it—some of the boys were shaking in their boots.

After that we had to steer in a zigzag route. Today is Sunday and we have had breakfast. We sighted land and we all cheered as we were out of danger now, and it was a relief when we landed safely in Liverpool at 2:30 in the afternoon of April 9th.

On the boat we were served hard biscuits and bully beef to last us on the train. We were the first of three Battalions to get off the ship, and it was delightful to set our feet on the soil once again.

We marched to the station and the train was ready for us. The boys all laughed at the train as it seemed so small and funny compared with the Canadian trains. After we were seated and packed in, we started out of Liverpool to our destination. The funny part about it was we didn't know when we left Toronto where we were going. The whole trip has been a secret. Every day we were guessing. The old country was beautiful after the snow we left behind us. They ordered us to stay on the train, and when it became dark to draw the blinds.

We stopped at Crewe Station and we rushed out, but were ordered back again. Next we stopped at Birmingham. There we were allowed to get off and have refreshments. There were quite a lot of people to welcome us, and they were pleased to shake us by the hand. We were ordered back on the train, and then we stopped at Bramshott. Well, we were rushed out and marched up to the camp, arriving at 5:00 a.m. Monday morning. Then we found huts to live in. No comfort, just the bare floor to sleep on. After unloading ourselves of the kit, we had to search for the wash house as we never had a decent wash on the ship. We found the washhouse but it was just a tap, no basins. After a while we had orders to fall in for breakfast, which consisted of tea, bread and a little bacon, which we were glad to get. The next thing was to find the YMCA. We found it, but it was not like the place in Toronto.

Anyway we passed the day looking around, but up to now we have no proper quarters. We had a muster parade Tuesday, and had a ten-mile route march. The village is small and we went down last night to get a good feed, as the food here is very poor. But the people here soak you so much for eggs and bacon.

I can assure you all the boys are longing to get their leave to have a good meal.

Well, I think my story is about ended till we meet around the fireside. Then perhaps we will be able to say more. So, goodbye for the present.

Your hubby,
Bert

Perhaps Bert's diary served to jog his memory for his letters home to Auguster: perhaps the letters inspired his diary entries. Whichever it was, there is sometimes almost word-for-word repetition between the two. This tells us that Bert was a careful diarist, probably a man who viewed the events around him with an eye and an ear tuned to their transposition onto paper. Bert's diary continues:

You could see joy in every eye, especially when we sighted Liverpool. After all that excitement, we arrived in Liverpool early in the morning on April 9, 1916.

Orders now came to have breakfast and secure rations for the train journey. We did not want telling twice. We all gathered up our kits. Our rations consisted of hard biscuits and some bully beef. The orders initiated pandemonium. It was no easy matter unloading over four thousand soldiers and their baggage. We all stood loaded up with full packs while two battalions disembarked. Finally, our turn came to put our feet again on the solid earth. It was a relief especially to those boys who had been sick the entire journey!

The next thing was to get on the train. The station was very near the docks. We marched over and lined the platform. Then, it was fun for the Canadian boys who had not seen English trains. They call the carriages "match boxes" and the engine a "jitney." It caused lots of jokes. We huddled into different compartments like sardines in a box, but we had a good time. After about fifteen minutes, we pulled out for our camp. We were still wondering where we would land again.

The troops of the Empress of Britain *had reason for concern on their voyage. Since November of 1914 German cruisers and U-boats had sunk over 185,000 tons of Allied shipping. In early September, on the eastern coast of Scotland, the German U-9 sank the British cruiser* Pathfinder *near the entrance of the River Forth.*

Later in the month German U-boats had a field day. Torpedoes sank the armoured cruiser Aboukir *in the North Sea just after she had parted company from her sister ships, the* Hogue *and the* Cressy. *The other cruisers saw that the* Aboukir *was in distress, and they went to her aid. As they approached the sinking ship, torpedoes from the hiding submarine ripped open the hulls of the* Cressy *and the* Hogue. *As the lifeboats were lowered to help struggling survivors, the gunners of the U-9 picked off the men one after the other like sitting ducks. All three cruisers sank in less than one hour with the loss of fourteen hundred British seamen.*

In March of 1915, a German U-boat attacked without warning a channel steamer named the Sussex. *It was carrying passengers from Folkestone to Dieppe. That U-boat made no effort to save the victims of its torpedoes.*

On May 1, 1915, the British liner Lusitania *left the port of New York City bound for Liverpool, England. Although she was carrying ammunition, the ship* was unarmed. On May 7, 1915, the Lusitania was approaching the coast of Ireland. Commander Walter Schwieger of the German submarine U-20 watched the Lusitania through his periscope. He ordered two torpedoes sent flashing toward her. Eighteen minutes after the first torpedo hit, the Lusitania was on the ocean floor. With her went 1,198 people, most of them civilians. There were 440 women and children on board, one hundred of them Canadian wives with their children, going to England to be closer to their husbands who were with the Canadian Expeditionary Force. Most of the 120 Americans on board were among the women and children.

Germany had not confined herself to International Law, which stated that prizes of battle be taken into port to have their status determined by a prize court. If Germany had played by the rules, she would not have sunk to the level of national degradation that now marked her.

HMS Empress of Britain. (Milly Walsh)

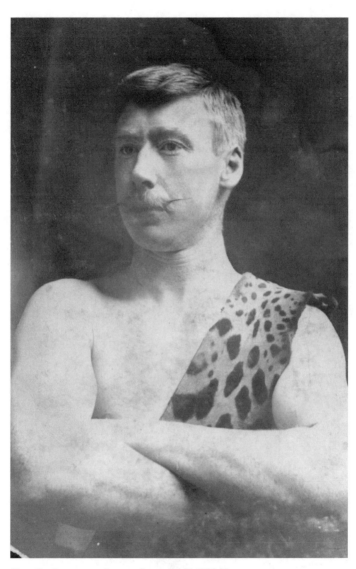

Bert Cooke in wrestling uniform. (Milly Walsh)

Bert Cooke in wrestling pose. (Milly Walsh)

CHAPTER 3

Bramshott Camp

Salisbury was a gigantic mudhole. At Bramshott it wasn't rats—or the bed-bugs or lice, it was the bloody mud!

As told to Lloyd Taylor by his father, Private George Taylor
(machine-gunner, 38th Battalion, 1916-1918)

The little engine that we laughed at started moving at such a pace that it surprised the boys. The beautiful scenery was an eye-opener for the Canadians. They thought England was so small and nothing like their country. Nevertheless, the boys were delighted with everything. Snow had blanketed the country we had left behind. This whole country was beginning to look green and beautiful.

Our first stop was Crewe, but we were not allowed to get out of the coach. Quite a few people cheered us on our way. By this time it was getting dark. It was about 8:00 p.m., and we were ordered to light up and draw the blinds.

After a few minutes we started off again. Every station we passed through people cheered us on our way. At Birmingham, which was very familiar to some, including myself, we received instructions to get out and have refreshments, which pleased everyone. We had to pay dearly for what we bought. People seem to think they are justified in charging the Canadians double the usual price. They say we have lots of money.

Many people welcomed us at this stop. The girls were eager to get a badge or something from Canada. Some of the boys had stripped themselves of all their badges, also some of the buttons from their coats. They would do anything for a kiss. We had a quite a time before we left that place.

Orders came to proceed, so we all boarded the train and continued on our way. The next place was the end of our trip. It was Bramshott Camp.

We arrived at the station at 4:00 a.m. April 10, 1916. Officers were waiting for us there to hustle us off the train. The transports were ready to load our kit-bags as we had about two miles to walk. The kits on our backs were enough. I can tell you our stomachs were about empty, and our load was very heavy.

After a few minutes, we commenced our march to camp. It was a very pleasant march, although it seemed a long two miles. The birds were singing, and the other smells and sounds of summer were sweet and pleasant. We had no band to play, but we whistled and sang till we reached camp. It was somewhat different to the camp in Canada. The huts looked bare and uncomfortable. We were about forty persons to a hut, but we were mighty glad to get our harnesses off and have a rest.

After unloading all of us, they told us that breakfast was ready. Like a shot we were off to the cookhouse to get something to eat. Our breakfast consisted of tea, bacon and beans and a little bread and butter.

After our march to camp, the next thing for us to do was to find out all about our sleeping quarters. We found out that we had to sleep for the next few days on the floor of the hut. The floor was dirty but not as shabby as the ship. At least windows could be opened so we could get fresh air.

The following is one of four poems Bert wrote while in the army.

Our huts they looked so nice and cozy after coming from the
    camp. With our faces good and rosy
and our shirts were very damp.
Our walk that day will never be forgotten. The man that led had
    little thought.

> He carried nothing on his shoulder but we carried all we owned.
> His pace was fast and nearly running till at last the men grew sick.
> One by one they started lagging, sure it was a dirty trick.
>   Bert Cooke

After a look around and asking a few questions, we learned that the rest of the day was ours. I took full advantage and started out to have a thorough look around our new home. First, I found the YMCA and the people there gave me the glad hand and the use of the rooms for writing and reading.

Naturally, I sat down at the writing table and commenced writing home. I wanted to let my friends know that we had settled down in our new camp.

Everything seemed strange around us. But, as soldiers we had to adapt ourselves to any place, plus the conditions facing us.

I spent a very pleasant day around the camp. Then, in the evening I took a stroll into the village of Liphook, which is about two miles away. By that time my appetite began to sharpen-up, and it was time to find a place to satisfy my hunger.

I walked around until I spied a garage. The garage was rented to a person for the purpose of feeding soldiers. Entering the garage, I called for ham, eggs and tea. The meal was a treat after being fed so poorly during the voyage. They charged me two shillings and sixpence for that meal. I was astonished! I thought it was three times as much as it should have been.

The people around the camp seemed to think that the Canadians are all millionaires. Never mind, I got over the shock only to be gypped again.

After a peek around the village I strolled back to our hotel at the camp for a nap. I stretched my rubber sheet on the floor, with a blanket on top. I used another blanket to cover myself. Believe me, although it was a very warm day it was chilly at night. I couldn't sleep. I just turned and twisted until I just had to get up and dress. I then lay down and tried to sleep for a while.

The next day was hot. After breakfast we were all called for a muster parade. It was a method to see if any of us had run away. All the boys were eager to get home to see parents or friends, but every man was accounted for after all the hustling around.

In the morning they dismissed us for our dinner. The command came to get on our packs for a route march. At 2:00 p.m. we fell in. Then, the band struck up a marching song and off we went. It was very hot and dusty, so you can imagine how we felt after a few miles of marching up and down hills.

Altogether we marched about ten miles. One thing for sure, despite it being a hard bed, I had no trouble sleeping that night. The same thing happened day after day. When nearing the end of the week we were expecting a six-day leave. It was what they called a landing leave. Disappointment came again. Packing up, we moved into other quarters on a Saturday afternoon. Being our half-holiday made it all the more difficult. They seemed to take advantage by doing stunts like that. You can imagine how we felt. Never mind, we're not dead yet!

We visited different towns nearby, and I had a very pleasant weekend. The thing I was looking forward to was my landing leave to go home. My wife Auguster and my two sons Morris and Harold had come back to England for a holiday. They had come back for the time that I was in the army. This way I would have a place to go when I got off on leave.

On Thursday we heard changes were going to take place in respect to the holidays we rightly deserved. It was arranged that the companies would leave the following Tuesday. The time came, and it was a jolly time. Being ready at 11:00 a.m., we managed to get away from camp and arrived at the station at 6:00 p.m.; not too long do you think? What do we care, we wanted to get on the train. We were not safe till we were on our way. They could change their minds and take us back to camp and fool us again.

After a long, weary journey, I arrived back in camp and settled down to work, repairing boots. Time went on and for two months the men drilled hard getting ready for the trenches. They were learning all the necessary skills to be ready at any time to answer the call.

That time came June 10 on a Saturday night. We were about to go to bed when the Commander ordered assembly. The bugle sounded for "A" Company, just before I had a chance to drop off to sleep. They started to examine the soldiers and were busy all night. Then, on Sunday permission denied to all as far as leaving camp.

It took about five days to get the men ready. Eight hundred men were picked to go away, then it changed to five hundred. By Thursday, June 15, they were ready to go. We had breakfast at 5:00 a.m. My name was down to go with this bunch, but at the last moment my name was scratched off the list. All my chums were going, so you can see how I felt.

At 7:00 a.m. the boys fell into formation. I will never forget the reaction of the men as they buckled on their kits. Some were jovial, but others with wives and families left in Canada were uneasy. You could see by the look on their faces; nevertheless they were right here. All rallied to the call, and fell in as the bugle sounded. I felt very broken up about my chums going away. Colonel Beckett, brokenhearted, tried to say a few words to the boys; but he could only say good-bye and turned away. Then the Chaplain offered up a prayer for the safety of the men. Every one bowed his head, and it was a solemn moment after that. The band struck up the tune of "Auld Lang Syne" and the "Maple Leaf." The order came to march off, and they all gave three cheers for Colonel Beckett. Then he stepped off with the soldiers.

Bert dedicated the following poem to the boys of the 75th:

When the call came from France for reinforcements the boys from our battalion answered, "yes!"

They buckled on their kit like heroes and said, "we will go like men."

When the bugle called the boys together not a murmur could be heard, every man was at his post Sir, fit and ready for the work.

Never shall I forget the day, boys when the Colonel stood in front to say a word of cheer to them.

But, alas his heart was heavy when he said, "good bye my men." Then the order came from four men, and our band began to play. Off they went with cheer and shouting from their pals who stayed behind.

They started singing "Rule Britannia," the "Maple Leaf," and "Auld Lang Syne." We all chipped in to make it pleasant as they marched off at a swing.

The sight will never be forgotten as those boys marched out of sight. You could see the tears a-flowing from the largest to the might.

We may never meet again boys on this earth of ours. But, alas we must meet yonder where there's peace for evermore.

Then we hope to see each other at the pearly gates up there, when our struggles will be over and at rest for evermore.

H.B. Cooke

I felt downhearted as the boys marched away. Perhaps, I would never see them again and the precious times we had together. A few days passed, and two hundred fifty extra men received the call. I was again on the list to proceed to France with these boys. I stood there with my kit packed waiting orders. I was ready to go right up until the last moment. To my astonishment my name was off the list again. I thought to myself perhaps it is all for the best. Once again I settled down to my work of repairing boots so the men could have something firm to walk in.

On June 18, the second draft was ready to move. They were the pick of the battalion, smart good-looking men. It seems a shame for such individuals to go over there and lose their lives to satisfy that cursed German militarism. Look out for the Germans that have to face our boys. They will show them the quality of the Canadian soldier.

The time came for the boys to move. It was not as hard to see them march away as it was the others, but the loss was felt deeply. I felt lonely; it seemed like being turned out from home. Colonel Beckett felt like a shepherd who had lost his flock. My thoughts were, what will they do with the few of us that were left?

News came that another battalion would split. We would have these men and retain our name as the 75th Battalion. That pleased Colonel Beckett and his staff.

One part of my story nearly escaped my notice. The story about our shooting which lasted ten days. We went on Saturday. It was a pleasant, six-mile walk to the firing ranges. The march was not easy as we had full kits, as well as carrying our rifles. Not used to marching, I must say how pleased I was to get to our destination. We found tents ready for us up on a hill. It was a beautiful spot, although it was dusty and sandy.

We arrived there in a happy and dusty condition, with our supper waiting for us. Despite our condition we were glad to get it. I think the army will cure a lot of these men who were so particular in home life. In my own case, it has done me a lot of good in this respect. A fellow learns to do more for himself than just mend holes in his socks. A man learns to cook, wash his own dishes and clean his own knife and fork. He learns a lot of other things that seem impossible to do when at home. It is great sport to see men doing these things for themselves.

Our stay at the firing range was pleasant. There's plenty to do and not much rest. We started on Sunday to go down to the butts to get instruction. The purpose was to prepare us for firing the next day. The heat was terrible. The sand seemed to draw the heat, but we withstood it. I had some exciting times there, as I undertook to do some butchering. I had to shoot too, but I would rather do butchering than some of the other work around the camp.

The washing conveniences are the worst thing about the camp. It was difficult to keep clean. Water was scarce. You would see persons washing in little pools, in ditches or any place they could find water. Only one spring supplied the whole camp. The sanitary arrangements were poor and some of the boys contracted diseases like measles and mumps.

After working arduously for ten days and our firing complete, I can't tell you how delighted we were to get back to our little home on Bramshott Hill. There we could have a bath and get clean after our experience at the firing ranges.

We all made up our minds to quit, and let the officers see that we are human beings, not cattle. Every man was all-in. Our clothes soaked with honest sweat from walking four miles and carrying about 80 pounds. I was glad that day ended when we came to our huts. I need more than pork and beans to keep up that pace. Never mind, we're not dead yet!

I must proceed with my story. After about two weeks from the time the boys went to the front, we heard that more Canadians had crossed the ocean. We were to get more men to make up the 75th once again. It was strange that another Toronto Battalion was coming to beef up our numbers. Those of us left kept the works going.

There was a lot of work to do at camp. The work generally rested on a few persons who were rather unfortunate enough not to know how to get out of it. You could see men dodging here and there to get out of the way. They would stow themselves away and have a nap till it was time to eat. Nevertheless, I had plenty of work as the men who went away left plenty of boots to repair.

It is nice if you could get home. I always dodged off at weekends and made tracks for Cirencester to enjoy the comforts of home as much as I could. A fellow must be able to take advantage when he has the opportunity. It was my one thought to live and to get home to Auguster and my two sons.

The food is so different at camp. Just receiving a parcel is good. Some of the men are like a lot of kids unpacking their parcels and rejoicing at their contents.

By this time we heard that our other men had arrived. They came on June 30, a Friday, arriving at about 11:00 p.m. The poor fellows looked all-in. They were hungry, but the men had to get their rifles first as we were expecting King George V to review the division the following day. It was hard on them, but they had to go. Dismissal came after about an hour. Everyone received a light supper after which they were ready to stretch out anywhere and have a nap.

The next day was the big parade and march. For every person it was mandatory. It was a long march about ten miles each way, but it was a grand sight to see about twenty thousand soldiers assembled and reviewed by the monarch. Before we got back, two of the men had to drop out of formation as the march was too much for them.

I had my share in the rehearsal about 7:00 a.m. The boys marched off and glad I was to see them go. I expected to be called out, but it was the waiting that made things sickening. I was looking forward to getting home, which meant a lot to me. I went off expecting opposition at the station, but was successful again and managed to get on the train.

I arrived back in camp the next night, tired but better for my holiday. It makes me feel better if it is only for the feed I got. At camp they don't care about giving us any dessert. We got the same old food all over again. The very sight of beans and stew would turn a hungry man sick after a home-cooked meal. I know for my own part, the sooner I get back to home life, the better, but we are in the army now. By this time our new boys are getting down to work, and we are about to move as a battalion of the 4th Division.

Bert now jots his thoughts down on paper. Another poem is fashioned that goes like this:

It is nice to look out of the window and see the troops marching by, and all the people watching the training of the men.

They work from morn till night Sir, and learn to bayonet fight.

You'd think it was fun to see them run and charge the dummy Hun.

But the day has come for our boys to fight.

They will do it too with all their might for in the 75th they teach them right, and I know they will chase them out of sight.

But don't forget they are running yet and will until the end.

Our boys are trained and far too well, they will drive the Germans on to Hell.

Bert Cooke

All the men are hard at work; even myself as a boot-maker. I have to go out and learn how to kill Germans. It seems terrible, but as the instructors tell us, "If you don't kill them they will kill you."

To give us some idea of trench life we spent a few days and nights in makeshift trenches. Everyone is getting spirited now. Everything is work from morning until night. We are all preparing to go to the front.

The Second Contingent arrived on British shores in the middle of 1915. That summer the Canadian government authorized the formation of scores of new battalions. More and more units were consequently dispatched overseas. Thus, Canadian camps spread to Witley, Seaford, Hastings, Bramshott, and other towns of southern England.

The Minister of Militia, Colonel Sam Hughes, had a simple view of recruiting: he wanted the largest army imaginable. A thousand recruits meant a battalion; half that made a cavalry regiment. In early 1916, he promised an army of twenty-one divisions, five of them from Toronto alone. British General Gwarkin, Chief of the General Staff, asserted that each division in the field needed between 15,000 and 20,000 new men each year. The urgent recruiting was the reason for canceled leaves and crash-course training at boot camps like Bramshott. The military staff wanted to get men into combat fast because the war in Europe was gaining momentum.

When the 4th Division reached the front line by September of 1916, all the Canadians formed their own army corps. With almost 100,000 officers and other ranks, the Canadian Corps had become one of Canada's national institutions.

The 75th Battalion was supposed to be a reserve unit. Little did Bert and the men of the 4th Division know that the world would soon recognize them as shock troops used as spearheads to pierce the tough parts of the German defenses. The question was, where would they be used first?

CHAPTER 4

To The Front

These men—the slaughter and the conditions that they fought under, they did-
n't want to expound on it, because they felt that nobody would believe them;
with the rats and the bugs crawling in their uniforms, the conditions—nobody
would believe them and it's hard to visualize anybody believing unless you
went through it. When you look over the parapet and you see all those little
red eyes and you suddenly realize they are rats—some as big as alley cats—
it's not hard really to understand [why a soldier did not want to talk about
his war experience].

Lloyd Taylor, son of Private George Taylor,
machine gunner, 38th Battalion, 1916-1918

In August of 1916, the Canadian Corps was brought up to what was from this
time on to be its full strength by the arrival of the Fourth Division in France. At
this date the first battle of the Somme was in full blast. The Canadians had no
part in the early stages of this terrible and prolonged struggle. It was not until
the beginning of September that the Canadian Corps was moved down to the
battle area, and not until the middle of September was the Corps engaged in
any serious action.

The date of my going to France August 11, 1916

Arrived in Belgium August 14, 1916

Two nights and one day we spent in boxcars. After the journey we started sleeping in barns and fields, watching men reap the harvest the old-fashioned way. We talked to the Belgians about their experiences and how they were treated. Finally, we started for the rest camp near the trenches, arriving there after a four-hour march.

August 16—We found some of our old boys and they were delighted to see us, 'A' Company and Bomber Signals. We went to our trenches, and during the night we had a gas attack so we had to put on our gas helmets.

I walked 16 miles to find one of my brothers and finally found him at a football match.

> On July 18, 1918, an article appeared in a Toledo, Ohio, newspaper. The headline read: Six Brothers, Four Years in Service, Win Service Pin For Toledo Woman. The pin was presented to the Toledo woman with the most near relatives in service. The woman was Bert's sister, Mrs. R. Maltman. The article concluded by saying: "All of the brothers have been wounded, sent home to hospitals and back again to the front line. One has been gassed four times."

August 19—I was transferred back to base to my old job of shoemaking. I did take a walk today to the place where my brother was stationed. We had tea and a friendly chat and then started back in the rain. Fortunately, we were able to catch a bus, but the ride back was on a very rocky road.

Halfway back to camp we saw people that had been forced from their homes. They were building little huts out of posts, mud and biscuit tins.

For ourselves we built bunks for sleeping to keep us off the ground. We would be a little warmer too.

Every house sells a few things, and the people are very conscientious workers. The dogs do a lot of work, working like little horses. The only thing to dodge work is the cat. They have the best time.

The roads, being made of cobblestones, are very rough. The beer is also very poor. We have great excitement with the gas helmets, playing games behind the firing line with no fear. Also, moving days are very frequent. Washing days are when you can get some water. In certain places you cannot get enough water to wash your face. We visited Poperinghe, Oudenaarde, Reningelst, Bocholt and Ypres, sightseeing along the way and having an excellent time. At the same time, we were always looking out for relics.

August 25—Our men went into the trenches relieving the 22nd French Canadians. Enemy shelling killed ten officers and wounded many as they entered the trenches.

Two of our men were blown to pieces. They picked up something they thought was a bar to lay across a fire for the purpose of making tea. But, these bars were deadly explosives and blew these two pals of mine to atoms and wounded several. They found minute body parts of the two men and put them in a small bag and buried them.

August 26—Today we moved from our transport line to take over the 22nd transport line at Reningelst five miles from the trenches. We walked about six miles, becoming soaked with rain. When we arrived we had to use a hut for a workshop and our sleeping place was a tent. We made special beds to keep us from lying on the wet ground. The dinner served consisted of bully beef and tea. We slept while the wind and sun dried our clothing.

You would laugh to see us looking for water. I have seen men washing in pools of water by the road side. Also, four or five men washing in a little water from a tin. The rats visited us in this camp. They were plentiful everywhere. It made no difference where we went.

As you pass along the road, you could see crosses stuck here and there. The names of some of our men were on those crosses, indicating their last resting place. We saw the names of many of our old boys that left us at Bramshott camp with the first draft. Lots of men were missing, and we were eventually informed of their death.

Our new camp was full of fun the first night. We wandered around the little town and found a place to have supper, which was served in a strange manner. The place was very dirty. Also, the people here live at a very slow pace and are very poor.

The people living in the private houses catered to the soldiers. You could see a card in most windows saying—eggs, coffee and chips. You had to sit down and watch them skin, cut and fry the potatoes. The coffee they had was in an old pot. The flies seemed to be as thick as dust.

The next thing I noticed was the funny way the blacksmith shod horses. It was a place just big enough for the horse. He would put a rope around the foot of the horse, wind it up on a bar, making it impossible for the horse to move.

When we got back to camp it was time to go to bed. When it became dusk it was virtually impossible to sleep, as the rats were putting on a performance on our tent. Those rats were chasing each other up, down and around the tent doing different stunts. It makes a fellow feel creepy when it's dark, simultaneously trying to get some sleep.

August 27—The morning finally came and it was a nice day. We commenced work—it being Monday morning repairing harnesses and boots, etc.

It was exciting watching our flying machines manoeuvre over the German trenches. Dozens of our machines drowned the enemy fire, and you could see the bombs bursting all around them. They seem to dodge the shells. It was paramount that we watch them.

All the activity at night is a glare as the stars and lights from both sides light up the trenches. The enemy always knew the nights our transports were moving provisions. Our transports had to be very careful as they were a reliable mark for machine guns.

August 28—After another night's rest we had a wet time as it rained early in the morning. Our artillery pounded shells into the enemy lines from morning till night. It was quite a sensation. It was perfect hell for them because you could see the dust, timbers, and bodies flying as you look toward their trenches. To make matters worse, a heavy thunderstorm came in the evening. The rain pelting down made conditions very uncomfortable. The water just poured down underneath your feet and soaked a fellow through to the bones. The rain did not stop us though. We just kept on firing away. We always waited for our chance to pop them off, and as quickly as possible.

Life in the trenches is a horrifying experience. Sometimes, as they stand by your side, your pals are blown to pieces, or they wind up buried in a blown-up trench. We scrambled out of those trenches but fast. One thing for sure, it is a nerve tonic for a man who is a little nervous.

Our visitors were the vermin and rats crawling over us. We needed to make ourselves as happy as possible. Occasionally a joke or two kept up our spirits.

When out of the trenches, you had to be on the alert all the time. You never knew when a shell would zoom your direction. Signs were even posted warning soldiers about snipers.

The shelling did not worry the boys. They played football and other kinds of games despite the shelling. War or no war, the sport must go on.

To help forget the sights, a fellow has to see something different. So, I would walk to some of the shelled towns and talk to people who had lost all of their possessions. It makes a person feel sad. In this part of the country, you had to be very careful who you talk to and what you say. The reason for this was because of all the spies.

Poperinghe was bombarded for four days. Accordingly, they discovered that the station manager was a spy. Because his telephone cable was connected with the German front line, relaying information was quite easy. They always knew what battalion was going into our trenches.

When we entered town the people welcomed the 75th Canadian Battalion. They promptly asked where the hell we were all coming from. We were not slow in telling them.

We had a feeling the Germans were short of food. We were convinced when we captured a German soldier. When we brought him into our trenches, he said he was famished. We gave him a loaf of bread and a tin of marmalade. He ravenously ate the lot and nearly consumed the tin containing the marmalade! He mentioned they were driven to fight and were afraid of the Canadians. Consequently, they were all willing to surrender.

It is wicked what they had to endure. Scores of men were chained to their guns. They relished the thought of being taken prisoner. Why? They knew they would be treated better in England.

Another experience out of the trenches was related to me by a buddy of mine. He told me last night what two soldiers on watch endured. The one soldier stood on a dead man. Three corpses surrounded the other soldier. Two of the three bodies lay sprawled on each side of him. The other body lay in front. The dead man in front had his guts all shot out. It surely makes a man toughen up when he has to see such atrocity.

Just before a charge, we would have a drink of rum. Then with fixed bayonets, courage, determination and unsurpassed doggedness, we had to scramble out of our trenches. The dirty work followed with our guns pouring out bullets at the retreating Germans. It is too much to describe!

August 30—During the night of August 29 we had another gas attack, but we were always ready.

After breakfast I went to a place where we had a shower bath. It was in a brewery in the village. There we were served with clean shirts and socks. It was the first time I had my clothes off for three weeks. It was a treat to have a bath and clean shirt.

After being newly washed we went for a nap. With the weather so unpredictable we get dirty repeatedly. We are knee-deep in mud in some places because of the rain. A person had to be very careful because the shell holes were full of water. If you did walk into a shell hole, it would be a rather repulsive bath and very uncomfortable.

During the night transports sank out of sight because the rain turned so many holes into mud.

The next morning brought a bright, sunny day. It was refreshing to get a little dry weather. The last day of the month was grand, and the roads were drying up.

The boys in the trenches were kept busy, but our guns had the enemy pinned down. Our boys had the range—given to them by the scouts who were doing fine work. After getting the range from one scout, the artillery demolished the whole lot of German transports.

The days are unusually quiet. It is the only time we could sleep as all the fighting is carried on at night. After dark, working parties headed back to collect food, water, ammunition and other supplies.

The journey in pitch darkness might take all night. Others repaired the day's damage to the trench. At dawn, the likeliest time for an enemy attack, everyone "stood-to" for an hour, peering nervously into the gloom.

Today was the first time the ration of rum was served. I can tell you, a portion of our poor boys needed it badly. They were soaked to the skin. Also, today we had jam-roll pudding for dinner. It was the first time we had this since I joined the army. It was quite a surprise for the men. You should have seen the lads smacking their lips. We got lots of tobacco and cigarettes also. A man will do anything to wear away the time and forget conditions. As we all desired to see the end, we received the news with joy about Poumanice [Rumania] coming into the war.

September 2—Saturday. A hot time in the trenches commenced as our guns shelled the enemy relentlessly. They responded occasionally, but we were going to attack at night. They always seem to know. At 11:00 p.m. our guns started to pound the Huns. Immediately they sent over a strong gas attack, but the gas was weak. Being wise to their tactics, our horns blew for miles around. Our bombs hit their targets, and Fritz's trenches were cut to pieces by our guns. We lost two men in the attack.

The Imperial Bank band in Reningelst played all evening as our guns kept time. The windows shook, and the skies lit up with gunfire. It makes one feel sorry for poor Fritz.

Our trenches are in a poor state owing to the rain. Parts of trenches are useable, but others run through houses. It is hard to know where the trenches start and end. When you are near them you would think it was just another field or woods. Our guns are all concealed. You could not tell it was a battlefield.

After an exciting night with two gas alarms we rose to find a pleasant Sunday morning. Breakfast consisted of hard biscuits, bacon and tea. We had no bread because it was very scarce.

As I write these few lines, a German airman attempted to get over our lines. Twenty-one of our planes, within fifteen minutes, came from the clouds and blew that Hun right out of the sky. The German air guns fired shells up at our boys as fast as possible. Our airmen dodged them all.

That afternoon we went to Dikkebus. Dikkebus used to be a good-looking town with its pleasant churches and stores. Today, the town exists as rubble. Not a house, church or store is left standing. You would think an earthquake had struck.

All the trenches are battered in for miles. A strange thought struck me, though, when the Germans shelled the church. Built on one of the walls was a crucifix. It was not touched. The tombstones are not even damaged. It is most remarkable and not a soul is left in town.

September 4—Monday. It is a quiet, brisk day with not much work to be done. I spent the evening chasing rats and reading. I crawled in for the night but could not sleep owing to those annoying visitors. Our visitors were the rats; gigantic, fat ones running all over the place. So, lighting a candle, I read a novel before dropping off to sleep.

As usual, the morning of the next day brought rain. Then we got orders to pack after having our breakfast of tea, biscuits and bacon. We were being moved to another camp; our winter quarters. So, after dinner we loaded our tools and kits. About 2:00 p.m. we started for our new quarters.

After about half an hour we arrived at our camp. The whole time it was raining. We waded about in the mud and water up to our knees. This place would have done well for ducks and pigs; they would glory in it.

We were told that it was better quarters, but conditions went from bad to worse. This time, we worked, ate and slept in a bell tent. Nevertheless, a soldier must adapt himself to anything. One comforting notion, it saved that cleaning of boots and buttons.

The move is our fifth in less than three weeks. We would do well as cartage agents after the war. This time we were a little better off; we had boards in the tent to sleep on instead of sleeping on wet earth.

Despite our living conditions, our guns continued sending Fritz a few "lead pills." We wanted them to know that we are still around.

While I sat in my tent, a band was playing "There Is Sunshine in Your Heart." Just then I failed to see the humour. The events happening around me are like a dark cloud. Every cloud is supposed to have a silver lining. I hope we see it soon.

It is fun watching the men when they arrived at a new camp. They would scrounge for anything that resembled a bed. It certainly made them more comfortable and kept them off the wet floor.

September 5—We spent a very miserable night. We were wet, dirty and not able to sleep for the blast of our heavy guns firing over our heads.

We rose the next morning, September 6, to find the sun shining and the birds singing. It was as if no war was being fought. To make things brighter, we were going to be paid. Nearly every man was broke. When the boys are broke, the boys are miserable. Before night came, some of the boys were more than happy and talked about their friends.

During the day's fighting, diverse men were wounded. One soldier had five bullets slam into his helmet. The impact knocked splints into his eye, which is very painful. He had to be dressed at the hospital.

Our boys made a charge at night but found no Germans in the front-line trenches. Those Huns always knew when there was going to be a bayonet charge. Consequently they would take off. Our guns continued unmercifully pelting them all night for several days.

We were having fine weather so I decided to have a walk around. I wandered into an enormous windmill to see how they functioned. They were on every hill. I discovered that these old-fashioned flour mills were driven by the wind. Four bins were used to put the wheat in to make fine flour. That accounted for the colour of the bread, which I often wondered about.

We had been trying to fix up a workshop the past few days. We would steal a bit here and there to help our building efforts. We captured a stove in the process. With all these things, we made a comfortable little place.

Because we were tired of biscuits and jam, I cooked ham and eggs for supper with tea for our drink. We thought we were dining at the Hotel Cecil instead of on the battlefield.

Another strange thing is that sometimes we were lost as to which day it was. Every day was always the same to us. Men gambled all day and all night. Others drank to drown their sorrows.

On the night of September 8, our guns roared all night. Under this barrage of shelling, the boys raided the trenches of those cursed Huns. We lost two of our officers.

On the fourth night, the Germans heard we were attacking again. On the attack our men were caught off guard; consequently our Third officer was killed. Nevertheless, we had the least casualties of any battalion.

Earlier that day, I saw five men who were cooking a meal for the 87th. Suddenly, you hear the whistling of a bomb; seconds later an explosion, I then see the body parts of all five men scattered about. One man had his head blown off.

Another of our boys tried to rescue one of our officers. As he was lifting him off the ground, a bomb exploded under the officer. The officer was killed instantly. The soldier escaped death suffering only shock. Very lucky!

It is awful seeing such horror happening all the time. When the men come out of the trenches for a rest, the first thing done is to cull out the men suffering from forms of battle fatigue or shell shock. When things are quiet, you hardly think a war is being fought.

Located in the trenches is the YMCA. It supplies us with the little things we needed. There is always a line-up of men, so we would sit around and tell yarns and read letters from home. We looked forward to the association more than anything.

That night we lost our Second Sergeant, a man named Rowly. He was a very active fighter and worker, so we were devastated by his death.

We had a break in the fighting, so we visited another town called Westouter. It is an old-fashioned place, with its old church and burying ground. That land had additional plots, aiding as a last resting place for a soldier.

The bar rooms are full of soldiers. As usual they try and drown their troubles and forget the war. A man I came in contact with told me he was tired of war as he had lost two sons a few weeks ago. That Sunday, women were dressed up and off to church. They were all the same religion, Catholics.

I placed a stove I had stolen in the workshop and managed to seize a few steaks and onions. I cooked them along with some tea I made. The band is playing "Nearer my God to Thee." I wish the band meant nearer home for me. It is wretched being so far away from home.

It makes a fellow feel glum to see all the young men marching off to the trenches. Perhaps I will never see them again.

The people will remember forever this country, the sights they have seen, and the military camps dotting the landscape. The countryside too was ravaged by the war. The women in black reflected that sorrow. It was a cruel picture in such a pleasant land with its splendid crops and rich soil, its old-fashioned houses and lovely walks. Now the country is in ruins, which will set them back years. But the situation seems to be brighter now.

September 10—Sunday. I visited the town of Poperinghe again, a larger town than the others. I saw some distinguishing wide streets with its hotels and churches, and a delightful market square. But like the rest of the places they were bombarded by the Huns. Several places were smashed, and nearly all the windows in the town were broken. The people living here seemed very downhearted.

The majority of the women made lace and sold it, very fine work indeed. The majority of their customers turned out to be soldiers, poorly paid ones at that. Consequently, nearly all the homes sold beer or novelties. This activity is their way of making a living.

The majority of the towns are headquarters for the different divisions. Those towns were full of all kinds of soldiers, and they liked to buy different paraphernalia to send home.

The sanitary conditions are not very exemplary in a town this size. The water used by the homeowners made repulsive odours as it flowed into the streets.

When coming out of the trenches, the soldiers had little difficulty finding places to go to for reading, food and bathing. Portions of a huge church are heaps of rubble. Also, near the town is a massive cemetery full of crosses. Hundreds of our brave boys are laid to rest here. Altogether it was a very interesting town.

Our fellows had a notable struggle the other day. Several times, different squads of our boys went in to the German trenches. We lost two officers in that encounter.

The next day five of our men asked permission of the Colonel if they could go out and get the bodies of the officers. The Colonel said he would not think of it. He concluded saying, "It would be murder to go out in broad daylight." These men had made up their minds to go. So, they got an officer to speak for them. The officer happened to be an engineer. The General did not approve of the scheme, but they told the General they were still going. The officer then said, "Come on boys," and they ran off up the trenches.

The Colonel gave orders to the rest of the troops to cover them. They ventured out into what they call "No Man's Land." Bullets and shells exploded and ricocheted all around them. One man was blown into a hole. Several times they were blown off their feet; finally, they got within a few yards of the German trenches, but the bodies were gone.

While the five men were in a bunch gathering up the officers' personal kits a shell dropped in the midst of them; sinking into the ground without exploding. Providence must have been with them.

It was a marvel watching those men gathering up all they could find. They ran zigzag to escape ricocheting bullets and managed to tumble back into our trenches without a scratch. They were met by the General and Colonel who patted them on the back. He said he had seen some daring dudes but none like that. Each man was recommended for the Distinguished Service Cross, and the outcome was just an act of Providence and nothing else. Only one of the men has since lost his nerve. While I talked to one of them about their experience, he said they were all practically senseless. No person could imagine what it was like as it was hell in the trenches.

"No Man's Land" is that space between our trenches and the enemy trenches. To venture into "No Man's Land," sudden death is your prime thought; the "Land" is littered with crater holes from the shelling and is full of barbed wire entanglement. Sometimes a rat would scamper along the top of the trenches. Even the rat got shot! None of the boys would kill the rats as they say they were company.

While we sleep, day in and day out, sometimes the rats would wake a fellow up by putting their frosty noses by your face. The rats would not take bites of you. They could tell whether you were alive or dead. For one thing, they are too well fed. They eat the dead bodies. You could see men's bones where the rats had eaten all the flesh off. You could even see where the men had been buried. Where the shell had dropped, the body was in pieces, then the rats would get a feed. It is a horrendous sight. Feelings of helplessness prevailed in trying to save a body. The shells were just too thick.

The last five nights have been very quiet, as they are getting ready for the Kaiser's birthday. We were planning a raid and bombardment for that date, and we were looking forward to seeing the results. I thought the raid would be a slaughter because our airmen deserted us too.

On September 12, the General of the 12th Brigade was wounded, as the Germans had located our headquarters and shelled it. A person never knew where the shells were going to drop. You were never out of danger. Sometimes it would rain shells and you would wonder where on earth they were all coming from.

The boys had some remarkable stories to tell as you walk down the trenches.

When mealtime came the men would stop firing. You would see them attempting to toast cheese or heat up some type of food. You could hear their cussed language in their endeavor. You would wonder if a war was being fought until a whiz-bang came over and blew part of your trench to smithereens. You knew then mealtime was over and it was time to start again.

We were about to move again from our quarters and get a few more miles up the line. We would just get settled, and then we would get orders to pack up and leave. It seems as though our officers did not like the staff to settle down and be comfortable. The move anticipated, the move home, never came.

September 15—We moved again to another camp right on the border of France. For the first time we had a fine day for moving.

Since it was a wet day yesterday, it made the earth very muddy to get about. We packed up in short order and got hold of a shafter of lumber. We put it down into a hole where the cart wheel went in. Two fellows pushed behind the cart to get the wheel out. I went flying into the mud. I pulled myself out and acted like a mule and pulled the cart into place. Loading the cart with all our kits and tools we continued on to find our new camp. We knew the name of the town, which was Loker. But on our arrival we could see no place that looked like our camp. We were shown our place, which was just a field. There we were, in an open field with no other accommodation, and the sky was our roof.

We had never been stuck for ideas. So, we got four posts and started building a hut. My mate stole the wood while I built the house. Dinnertime came, but no food in sight.

We had no more stuff to use. Our shack was only half built, so we decided to lie down. Getting a little downhearted, we had a little rest. While resting, we discussed how we were going to find roofing materials. So, I went off and found some sheets of iron. I put them up, and my pals went scrounging to find a few more boards. We were then stuck for nails. I got those from the blacksmith. With a few boards and bits of tarpaper, we got that shack of ours built.

Beds for our hut was the next thing. We wanted to make a workshop out of it as well. So, we built three beds on top of each other. This way we had room to crawl in. With the beds finished, we installed a stove, which we had stolen. The stove went in the corner. Very soon we had a fire going. We tried to make the shack as comfortable as possible.

By this time I was becoming tired. So, I took off my clothing without too much trouble and tumbled into my cot near the roof. It was a pleasant feeling to lie down and hear the fire crackling. After a little conversation about our day's works we dropped off to sleep. For once, that night we had a decent rest away from the rats.

The next morning I woke from my slumber. The sun was shining through our newly made window. It certainly was a lovely morning. We said to ourselves when we got up, "We must capture something to cook as we must have food." Eventually breakfast consisted of a biscuit, slices of bread, bacon and a little tea.

After breakfast we went out stuffing up the draft holes in our hut. So, cutting sod segments from the field we put them on the roof. Obtaining a few more boards, we were able to complete our new home. Before night I was fairly comfortable. We made our own tea and had the best meal I had partaken of for a long time.

By the end of this second day, which was September 16, I was desperately in need of a wash and shave. Finding a little water, I heated it up and accomplished my task.

In the evening, I took a stroll around to see the town. The town is quite sparse, with four tiny, short streets. Nearly every house had a store. Only one of those stores served as a brewery. As usual, this town had a Catholic Church. I went inside to find it all lit up with candles. A service was going on but very few people were in attendance. It took me less than ten minutes to see all of the town, so I took a ramble into the countryside and soon found myself in France.

The country around here was elegant with its hills and valleys so green and the trees in all their splendor. All around the hilltops were the old windmills and the women working in the fields. All through the countryside, you would see a few old men building little houses. If the soldiers were not present, you would wonder whether a war was actually being fought.

I got back to camp in good shape. After a little conversation, I tried to get some sleep. I was informed that there was going to be a heavy bombardment all along the line. Consequently sleep was farthest from my mind.

At this point we have artillery all around us as we are very near the trenches. It was a pleasant moonlit night and about one o'clock in the morning the guns removed that pleasantness. It was unbearable to lie in bed. The whole sky was afire with bright flashes from the artillery shells. For half an hour the sky was littered by the shells' debris. Our guns pounded the enemy trenches relentlessly. The effects were seen for miles. The whole earth trembled. What the Germans thought I have no idea. But the majority would never know what hit them.

It is now Sunday. We will get a little news. One of our runners told me that we had eight casualties, a single man killed and seven wounded. Adjustments were made at various points along our line of defense. Consequently, batches of Germans were captured. Unspecified numbers would not relinquish and had to be killed. I was unable to gather more information.

That beautiful sunshiny morning, our airmen had German airplanes in their gun's sights. Our air guns exchanged fire with them. They never hit one another because our men knew how to dodge German machine-gun fire.

While the air battle continued above us, a farmer was in his barn only a few yards from us threshing corn. The threshing machine in the barn had no engine. So, he was out beside the barn using two horses. The horses were harnessed to a long shaft and were walking in a continuous circle to drive the machine.

It seemed that the Germans took any machinery the Belgians had away. Also, when they were in these towns they bought nothing. They did give the people promissory notes. They said they would pay after the war, but we knew differently. We were so different, as we paid for what we got. Numerous people were making lots of money out of our men. We taught them how to fry eggs. They say they never but boiled them before the Canadians came into this country.

The majority of people speak English very well. All the shops were open Sundays as well as all week. Every day seemed about the same to us. Consequently, it was very difficult to know the exact day.

The weather favored the farmers during the past week. Nearly all the grains are in, and they are now picking the hops and tobacco. Due to the very rich soil they are able to grow quantities of both the hops and tobacco. Just when the farmers harvested one crop, they put in another without wasting any time. I must say the few people that were left worked slowly but surely.

After fighting twenty-six days, our boys came out of the trenches to go to a rest camp. The last night was the liveliest they ever experienced. It became the biggest night's work for the artillery.

I was talking to some of the boys and getting their stories of the fight. They said our artillery fire was a wonder. They swept No Man's Land. Our machine-gun fire sprayed the whole of the German lines with bullets. Before making the attack, the infantry dashed out of our trenches. So, it was easy work for them to capture quite a few prisoners. Certain individuals would not surrender, and they all got what was coming to them.

A case I heard of was when an officer of ours captured a German officer and seven other Germans. They were asked to surrender, but the Huns said no. The German officer told our officer, "Go to hell!" and would not come. So our officer shot the German and found on him most valuable papers and a four-month diary. We had very few casualties all along the line.

It rained again, and mud was up to our knees. Nothing saps the soldiers' morale more than this ever-present gumbo. Even the strongest boots had their seams wrenched apart by men's efforts to struggle out of the mire.

Our little shack let in rain. So, to be able to work we dug a drainage trench in our hut.

We had to repair boots with our puttees in water and mud until we really could not see them. Without doubt every man had to lace up his boots very tight or lose them in the mud.

We have better food now because we are cooking our own. I cooked steak and bacon and made supper for two nights. I made pancakes for the boys, and it seemed like home without home comforts. Three of us were having a terrific time of it.

It was about 8:00 p.m. the evening of September 18 that new orders came. We had to be packed and ready to move on September 19 into

France. Before going to bed, I thought I would cook a little late supper. So, I made tea, cooked some bacon and ate at 11:30 p.m.

I went to bed but awoke at 2:15 a.m. in the morning. When I got up the rain was pelting down again. After all, it was our moving day. I made a fire and started to get breakfast. After having breakfast at 3:00 a.m. in the morning, we started to pack up. Loading our kits, we were ready at 6:00 p.m. to start our three-day march. It was not until about 8:30 p.m. that the battalion was ready.

The weather was pleasant now. The rain had cleared, and the sun was shining.

It seems that the troops never fully understood their role in the overall battle plan. The strategies were well established in the minds of the generals directing the battles, but for the troops, fighting was fighting. It made no difference where the fighting took place. The battles they fought might have appeared insignificant to them.

Only when reminiscing did the men realize the importance of the battles they fought. The only exception would be the conflict at Vimy Ridge.

On September 15, the day that Bert and the 75th moved to another camp right on the border of France the Canadians experienced their first important battle approximately twenty kilometres to the south. They were engaged in the capture of Sugar and Candy trenches near Courcelette.

As the 75th woke up to a new day—September 16—their comrades to the south reached the outskirts of Courcelette and captured the sugar refinery. This action is notable not only for the fierce fighting involved but for the fact that for the first time tanks were used in cooperation with the Canadian infantry.

Six battalions of the 2nd and 3rd divisions attacked and eventually captured the village of Courcelette. Monquet Farm was taken by the 1st Division, and several other minor gains were made. It was one of the neatest and most clean-cut campaigns of the Somme. Of this success, a memorable feature was the dashing attack of the 22nd Battalion, the French-Canadian "Van Doos," proving themselves on this occasion a true cousin of the impressive infantry of

France. For days the Germans strove stubbornly to retake Courcelette, but their efforts resulted only in further loss of ground and further punishment.

It is difficult to say when trench raiding by night began on the Western Front. But, in the development of the art of raiding enemy trenches the Canadians have a good claim to be regarded as pioneers.

The woodcraft that most Canadians knew from childhood, gave them an advantage in the midnight encounters between trenches.

Early in November 1915, the Canadian staff concluded that strong ninety-man raiding parties could enter the enemy trenches, inflict damage and casualties out of all proportions to their own losses and get away with prisoners.

Men with blackened faces, armed with clubs, knives, and grenades, would sneak out cautiously through a gap in the barbed wire to patrol No Man's Land. They would try to capture Germans for the information they could give. The slightest sound might bring a rush of machine-gun fire, or an artillery barrage that would light up the sky with flares and rockets.

Men routinely spent a week in the trenches rotating between three lines. In the fire trench men sought shelter from the rain in shallow "funk holes." These holes were carved in the wall of an eight-foot trench. A protruding foot or hand of a man buried in trench walls might even be used to hang a haversack.

Farther back, dugouts provided dank odorous shelter. Sometimes these shelters had bunks made from scrap lumber and chicken wire. Most of the time, a man would just lay his waterproof sheet on a bare mud floor for sleeping. There was seldom any system of ventilation to blow away the reek of unwashed bodies, wet serge, rotting food and stale urine.

Trench mats—"bathmats" in the soldiers' vocabulary—made of slatted wood like ladders were supposed to keep the men's feet above the mud. But these were soon swallowed up. In some places, three layers of mats were dug up, the earliest having been laid by the French in 1915.

Rations arrived in sand bags. When unpacked, the sugar and loose tea leaves would be hung from the walls of the trench, cans of stew and corned beef and the notorious plum and apple jam would be piled underneath, and *stacked on the top lay army bread or hard, dry biscuits. Once emptied, the bags were filled with earth to form trench walls and ramparts.*

Most soldiers agreed, although there were exceptions, that artillery bombardments were the most terrifying experience of all in the trenches. Even the bravest man broke down as the earth trembled and shook.

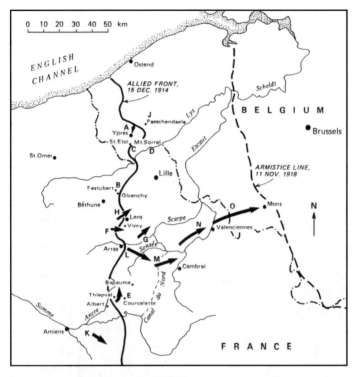

A   The Battles of Ypres, April-May 1915

B   The Actions at Festubert and Givenchy, May-June 1915

C   The St. Eloi Craters, March-April 1916

D   The Battle of Mount Sorrel, 2-13 June 1916

E   The Battles of the Somme, September, October, November 1916

F   The Battle of Vimy Ridge, 9-12 April 1917

G   The Battles of the Scarpe, April-May 1917

H   The Capture of Hill 70, 15-25 August 1917

J   The Battle of Passchendaele, 26 October-10 November 1917

K   The Battle of Amiens, 8-11 August 1918

L   The Battle of Arras, 26 August-3 September 1918

M   The Canal du Nord and Cambrai, 27 September-11 October 1918

N   The Capture of Valenciennes, 1-2 November 1918

O   The Final Advance, 3-11 November 1918

Poperhinghe, Belgium. (Milly Walsh)

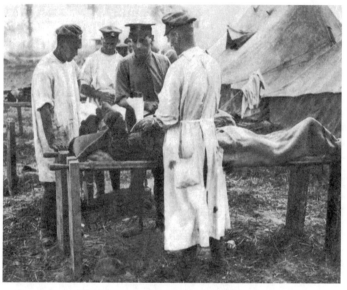

Arthur Cooke (foreground), twin brother to Ralph Cooke, administering First Aid. (Milly Walsh)

A typical First Aid truck. (Milly Walsh)

Top: The YMCA Canteen dugout situated one hundred and fifty yards from the Boche Lines. (The John A. Hertel Co. Ltd., Toronto, 1919)

A mule-drawn cart used in the First World War. (The John A. Hertel Co. Ltd., Toronto, 1919)

CHAPTER 5

On The March

You don't hear many historians praising the Germans, but they should be praised. They were as good as most of the Allied troops, and they didn't give up easily. You had to kill them.

Lloyd Taylor, son of Private George Taylor,
machine-gunner, 38th Battalion, 1916-1918

We arrived at Bailleul at 10:35 p.m., a very pleasant town. Parts of town are admirable, other parts old-fashioned. The town's cobble roads made it bad for walking. Groups of people stood gazing at us as we passed through town. We eventually had to rest for dinner at 12:30 p.m. just outside Strazeele.

After an hour rest we started off again only to halt for fifteen minutes. A motor truck slipped off into a ditch blocking the road. Then, a pack mule became over-balanced and rolled into the ditch. Several men had also fallen out of the march. One man fainted, but the doctor was able to bring the soldier around. So far, the people in France seem more sociable.

We halted for the night at a place called Hazebrouck. It is a quaint town. We arrived there about 5:00 p.m. with rain still pelting down.

The battalion went into different billets to sleep. Some slept in a deserted hospital, others in barns and schools.

The boys and I washed and cleaned up after being served supper. We then took a stroll around town.

We sampled drinks from the French bars and visited different stores to get eats. All the people seemed glad to welcome the soldiers, especially the bar maids!

After looking around, I wandered back to find a place to sleep, but could only find a place in one of the passages of the building. Being tired as a dog, I pulled off my boots and lay down on the cement floor by the wall, wet clothing and all. I only slept for about an hour because I was shivering too much. As a result, I would sit up during the night and eat a hard biscuit in an effort to warm myself.

I tried sleeping again after about an hour. For once, I was glad when it was time to rise. I was just like a piece of ice.

Finding the path to the field kitchen I revived myself with a warm pot of tea. Along with the tea I had a piece of bread and fat bacon.

The morning came with orders to get ready to start on our second day of marching. We started off about 7:15 a.m.

After marching about a mile out of town, we waited for about an hour before the other battalion was ready.

We continued walking until 12:15 p.m. before halting for dinner. Tea, biscuits and bully beef were served. I can assure you we were thankful.

We now got permission to lie down and rest for a while. The terrible part was getting up to march off again because marching on cobbled roads stiffened our legs. It is not like walking on a smooth level road.

The march went well, and we arrived at Arques, which was already occupied by our troops. It is an ancient town with a river flowing through it. The military authorities used the hotel for headquarters because it was the most modern and largest building. An immense square looked like a market place. Since we had easy access to the whole area, all our transports pulled in to for the night.

We arrived in Arques at 3:00 p.m. in the afternoon. Our men billeted out to any place where room was available—tables, hen houses, back yards, and any old place. We spent the rest of the day washing our feet. We were also looking around for those who could walk. Certain individuals could not walk and were content just to lie down and rest.

After sleeping soundly that night, we got ready to march off again. We started out about 7:30 a.m.

We passed a Catholic church with its graveyard laden with tombstones. We saw some funny effects. For example, huge glass cases covered some of the graves. The people used all kinds of decorations on the graves as well.

Off we went again to the rest place. We passed through St. Omer, a pleasant town with five immense churches. St. Omer was more modern than the other places.

After we passed through town, the beautiful countryside was quite noticeable. The scenery was dandy, with all its hills and valleys. The people were pleasant, quite different from the Belgians. The weather and the roads were perfect, but our poor feet were certainly not! Nevertheless, we continued our march through the countryside, with its birds singing, and the cattle grazing. The farmers were tilling the land as if no war ever existed.

We halted for a rest at a place called Ardres. Every place we stopped, women and girls gathered around us carrying their baskets filled with plenty of food to sell. They would walk for miles to sell their lot. Generally, they managed to sell out and go home joyfully.

We trudged on, marching up and down hills on the Calais road wishing for dinnertime so we could have a rest. We continued on though, and passed through another town called Tilquis. Tilquis is a tiny place, situated on a hill with a few old houses and a hotel. That made it easy for us to go down hill, as we would rest at the bottom.

Since it was 12:00 noon, we all thought it was dinnertime. The men had orders to feed the mules. Before having a chance to sit down we had orders to move again. Buckling on our packs, we continued on our way grunting and grumbling. After thirty-five minutes we had orders to rest and get dinner. Forty minutes was the time allowed for dinner. So, we sat down and received hard tack and bully beef, but it was a drink we needed and not a man had any in his bottle.

After a while a water cart came along. I managed to get a little drink for which I was thankful. Then, I stretched out on the grass and was soon in dreamland. The nap did not last long as a nudge on the shoulder woke me up to march off again. We continued on to our destination where the brigade is to have a few days' course in fighting.

We arrived there about 2:00 p.m., weary, footsore and ready to drop. We had to billet in an old dilapidated house. Tea was waiting for all and we were glad to get it. After that, I lay down under an old apple tree and fell asleep for an hour. After my nap I then wandered around to find out the name of this place. It is called Nort-Leulinghem.

Altogether, we walked about fifty miles in three days. We unpacked our tools with our other paraphernalia and took them into an old house. We then had to find a place to sleep. So, I went out and stole a bale of straw lying by a rack of wheat. I brought the straw into our old place, and spread it in the corner. The straw was dripping wet, so, I put my oil sheet on top of it. Lying down on the sheet, I soon fell off to sleep with no cares. Being exhausted I could have slept on clotheslines!

Morning came, and we had some work staring us in the face. Nearly every man in the battalion needed their boots repaired. It made no difference that it was Sunday; we had to get busy and fix the boots. From early morning until late at night we hammered away. We hammered for three whole days until we had the men's boots all fixed.

The people here were very upright. They would give us beer and are very sociable.

In the public houses, they charged us only one penny for a glass of beer. In Belgium they charged us double. So, you can really see the difference in people.

This part of the country is very pleasant, and the band played every night at the corner of the street. It was enjoyable to hear the music.

During our stay here the Brigade had been practicing open fighting for the Somme. Many different points had to be learned.

Also, we had been very busy repairing boots. A thousand pairs of boots went through our hands the ten days we have been here. We worked almost night and day to get the men's boots fit for another march.

We had also spent lively times at night as we drew our money and spent it on liquor. Several men suffered being caught drunk. They had seven to fourteen days of punishment including being tied to a tree for two hours a day. They had to do several other duties as well.

It was the last day of our stay, and we were vigorously preparing for tomorrow's nine-mile march.

October 3—It was no easy task getting the battalion outfitted, and the transports loaded. A fair amount of bickering went on before the task was done. Finally, we started off again.

It was impossible to get a change of clothing. Because we had to sleep on straw and in old barns, a person could not help getting lice. You could see every man daily with their shirts off picking out those lice. We tried disposing of them as fast as possible. They made fun catching them. One louse I saw was as large as a fly.

After our stay here, we received orders to move on to the Somme. We loaded up on the morning of October 4, and we walked about eight miles to the station. It was a stiff walk, up and down hills and hard roads. We passed numerous camps and pleasant country along the way. Certain individuals dropped out of rank with sore feet. My feet were hurting enough. Because I was traveling with the transports, I could hop a ride whenever I needed one.

We reached the station about 11:00 a.m., tired and hungry. The only food we had for the day was one slice of bread per person and a little tea. It's not enough food for men on the march.

We arrived at the station before the troops, as we had to load our wagons and horses. While the party loaded up, I scurried around to find some stores to buy food. It was like trying to find money.

The troops wound up in boxcars, and a bunch of us had to ride on the open trucks with the wagons. It was very cold with the night in front of us. We pulled out of this place, a town called Andechy, at 2:15 p.m. in the afternoon. We had a pleasant time until night came. Then, it became damp. We had to try to sleep lying down in that wetness.

We traveled for twelve hours on that train! The ride finally ended about 2:00 a.m. in a pleasant town called Ham. It was dark, so we were unable to see much at all. Nevertheless, after getting off the train we prepared for a three-mile march to another camp. Before starting out, I managed to find a place to get a cup of tea and cake.

We had some disastrous experiences as the troops moved out in front of the following transports. We had to travel on defective roads and under an avenue of trees that made it darker still!

Once, we encountered a steep hill. The kitchen-wagon mule team jibbed and backed into the ditch, holding up the whole bunch. None of the mule teams could get up that hill. Consequently, we had to double the teams. It took us over one hour getting up that hill and it nearly exhausted us.

We started off for camp and arrived at Goyencourt at 6:00 p.m. We pulled into a field that was like a mud pit. The troops billeted in old, broken-down barns. The barns were also full of livestock, but anywhere will do when a man is tired and weary. We wandered about trying to find places to sleep. I slept in an old wagon.

Orders came the next morning to pack up and move again. We departed Goyencourt at 9:30 a. m. After marching through several tiny villages, we reached rest camp. Rest camp looked inviting to us along with the tents they supplied for us. After our meal we lay down for a rest and some badly needed sleep.

The next morning, we had to move again. We started out about 9:00 a.m., marching an additional ten miles despite having sore feet. We arrived at a place called Contay. It was a town full of hospitals and headquarters. Consequently, very few citizens occupied the town because of all the soldiers.

For some of the boys a few huts for sleeping were located in a huge wooded area, but it was knee deep in mud. Because of the morning sun, I lay down in the open field with a little canvas over my head. I thought I was going to get a decent kind of sleep. But, I was soon awakened by the rain pouring as if it had not rained for years. The next night I put my rubber sheet down on the ground on top of some wet wood. Covering myself with half of my rubber sheet, I lay down and said, "Let it rain." No rain came at all that night.

We worked at repairing boots out on the hillside, and it would have made some picture. We stayed here in Contay for two days then we left for another destination. We reached the village of Albert on October 10 after marching seven miles.

At one time, Albert was a likable town but today it is a wreck. Not a house remained intact. A predominant sight to see was the vestige of a beautiful church. The church stood in a leaning position on a hill. Considering the church's condition it was quite a sight.

We were in the chalk hill area around the town where the Germans had been forced to retreat. From here the men had gone to the Somme's front.

The afternoon of October 11, the boys marched off in small parties of fifty at a time a little distance apart. Our band played them off sending them away in jovial spirits. Little did they know where they were going. Nevertheless, they marched off with no thought that they were going to a picture show. Before going far, they knew they were in for an exciting time. They realized too they would see sights never before witnessed. Guns were positioned to the right, and to the left of them. With the guns blasting all around, it is reminiscent of thunder.

Walking through the German trenches, I stepped over dead bodies strewn on both sides of the trenches. The majority of the bodies were not buried. The bodies that were, were only half buried with legs protruding out of the ground. It was a sight a fellow does not want to see again.

Little mounds marked by crosses cluttered the landscape. Inscribed on the crosses is the phrase "Rest in Peace."

The country around us is full of shell holes and smashed trenches.

The dugouts were a marvel. Certain dugouts were like a palace with electric lights, easy chairs and beds. Sprawled on several beds lay dead Germans, killed like rats in a hole!

October 16—The Huns shot a few shells into the village of Albert killing one of our officers. Also, two Germans tried to invade our lines in aircraft. Our airmen were around them like a swarm of bees blowing them and their aircraft right out of the sky.

October 21—Just above our camp, one of our airmen started having trouble. He was a long way up when his engine started acting funny. He tried to do all he could to make a clear landing, but plummeted into a tent, nearly killing a soldier occupying the tent. The machine finally came to rest crosswise in a new trench. The airman escaped with slight injuries.

Our boys made an attack on the German lines the same day. The artillery started shelling in the morning. Our men attacked Fritz at noon, taking their objective. They also seized the ridge post, which included five hundred prisoners. The men did well because in some places it was knee-deep in mud and water. Mr. Fritz is gratified to be taken prisoner.

The night of November 6 I will always remember. About 9:15 p.m., just as we were about to turn in for the night, Mr. Fritz started bombarding the town. For about two hours we had a fiery time of it. Luckily, no one was killed, and only four were injured. Our boys came out of the trenches for a rest.

November 10—Today we had to walk to a little town called Bouzincourt, where we were billeted in barns and houses. We were well fed after resting two days. We then had orders to get ready for the trenches.

The Somme was the training ground for Vimy—but at the cost of twenty-four thousand Canadian casualties. The worst experience came in October with the Canadian assault on the Regina Trench. But, would the battle for the Regina Trench be an Allied victory or a German victory?

The first battle of the Somme was fought between July 1, 1916, and November 1916. Its purpose was twofold: to achieve a breakthrough in the line and to relieve pressure on the French, who were defending Verdun to the south. By the time the fighting petered out the following winter, gaining nothing but possession of a few acres of ground, all four Canadian divisions had been blooded. The first three divisions fought from September 3 to mid-October when they went north to the Vimy front. The newly created 4th Division stayed on the Somme from October 10 to the end of November when they joined their comrades at Vimy.

What is loosely described as the Battle of the Somme, was actually a series of battles, an assortment of ghastly setbacks and minor victories.

It was an attempt to put into effective practice the lessons of warfare learned from the first year and a half of the war: the massing of artillery, limiting objectives to one, and the use of the barrage.

When the Canadians reached Albert, where they concentrated for their share of the Somme offensive, they had little chance to practice new roles or even to check on the ground. Conscientious military staff worked feverishly to get thousands of men and their guns, ammunition and supplies into position, leaving them no time to survey, rehearse, or understand their mission.

On October 17, after a little over a month, three shattered Canadian Divisions withdrew to refit in a quiet sector in front of Vimy Ridge while the new 4th Division had its turn. Men paid the price of inexperience in what was to be known as the battle of Thiepval Ridge.

As the bitter winter of 1916–17 swept down on Europe, the 4th Division tried again. The heavy Somme mud had made the problem of the attacking troops heartbreakingly difficult.

With help from the 10th Brigade, in snow, sleet and a wind that blasted straight from Siberia, they succeeded in capturing Desire Trench, which was the German support line.

The Regina Trench, the German defense line north of Courcelette was in Allied hands on November 11, 1916.

In one month of fighting the Canadian Corps had sustained 29,029 casualties for a mere six kilometres (about four miles) of mud.

The Canadian Corps had now attained the strength of four divisions. In the fighting about Courcelette, Regina and Desire trenches, the men of these four divisions and their commanding officers had gained valuable experience, experience that would serve them well in their next battle, Vimy Ridge.

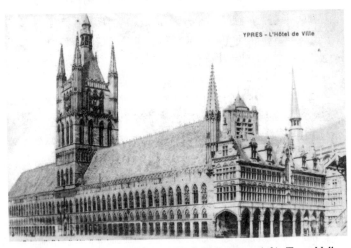

Ypres, Belgium. Belfry (back left), Cloth Hall (centre left), Town Hall, and L'Hotel de Ville (right foreground). (Milly Walsh)

CHAPTER 6

Back to the Trenches

It was just a slug fest. It was Currie that told them, 'We're going to take Vimy' and they did—by noon hour. The world just shook their heads. The Canadians—who the hell are they? That should be taught in our schools.

Lloyd Taylor, son of Private George Taylor, machine gunner, 38th Battalion, and a survivor of the battle at Vimy Ridge on April 9, 1917.

On November 13, groups of men were put into motor wagons and taken part way to the trenches. They were served out with rubber boots and fur jackets. This time, they have to advance into the trenches.

The night of November 15 the transports had to stock up on rations and water. During that time we had four horses killed, and a single man had his leg blown off.

On November 16 the Germans shelled us, dropping shells all around the house where we were working, killing several men and eight horses. We had a lively time for about an hour. Everything went well until the evening, when our transport lost four horses going up to the front line with rations.

Today I celebrated my thirty-sixth birthday in Albert; every thing went well until after supper. Mr. Fritz started to propel a few more shells at us. The shells exploded so close that shrapnel was falling on our old house. We scampered fast into the cellar! Thirteen of us hid in this tiny wine cellar until the bombing had finished. Fritz is not particular where he sends his bombs!

I went to bed, sleeping until about two the next morning. When I woke up, I heard the German airships busily dropping their time bombs. I finally rose for breakfast when an explosion suddenly rocked our house. Then, several other bombs went off, wrecking several houses and the ordinance stores.

After breakfast I walked in to the trenches to fix boots for the boys. Our battalion was in the trenches ready to make a charge.

November 18—At 5:30 a.m. they made a successful dash, but lost heavily owing to a little mistake by another battalion. One major and five other officers were wounded. Also, scores of men were killed and wounded. We did gain our objective, capturing four hundred prisoners besides doing tremendous damage to their troops. Our boys fought like heroes, fighting up to the waist in mud and water.

After being in the trenches for six days we got replacements. Tired and worn out, we wandered in to Albert, a distance of about eight miles. We were told that the next day we would move away from the Somme.

We had an order that all men were to be sent up the line again for working parties. I must say you could not see a smile on any faces.

Before the men returned, we had orders to move again. So, on November 26 at 11:00 a.m., we left Albert.

After walking ten miles we reached Lëalvillers about 6:00 p.m., tired and exhausted. Several men went in barns, but I wound up sleeping in a tent on a wet, muddy floor with no supper. So, laying down my rubber sheet, I stretched out with all my clothing on and tried to sleep. Although I was tired, it was too cold to sleep. About 1:00 a.m. I got up and soon got a fire underway. After warming up, I made a little tea.

During the day we got busy fixing boots. In the interim a portion of the men went out on working parties. We were to stay here for three days, so we were looking forward to finding a place for the winter.

November 30—The weather for marching today is fine but it is very cold. We started walking again and after a twelve-mile march arrived in Doullens at 3:30 p.m. It was a pleasant town, and the people were very kind to us. Getting into a town to see some life was a treat. We billeted in various sheds, but I went to a house and had a comfortable bed that was very acceptable.

We were on the march again after only one night of rest. The weather for marching remained dry and cold. So, before leaving I had a hefty feed of eggs and coffee. We had to keep a steady pace, because it was a sixteen-mile hike to a tiny farming village called Oeuf. We arrived about 3:30 p.m., exhausted and chilled. There we were put in barns and sheds. To keep warm it was necessary to curl up in the straw. After an hour passed by, supper was served. Then, we all went to roost.

The following morning we set off again for another ten miles. It was a little easier marching, but the roads were getting worse because they were wet. Those wet roads really made the walking difficult and the feet very sore. By this time various men had severely sore feet. My feet were beginning to feel the worse for wear as well, but I had to keep on going.

We finally reached our destination for that day about 1:00 p.m., giving us all afternoon to rest. We were put in barns and sheds again. As usual, it was up to us individually to get straw for bedding.

After resting for another night we had another march in store for us—about fifteen miles. It turned out to be my worst day because my feet were extremely sore, and I had such a severe cold. I hardly knew how to walk with my bag on my back. I could hardly get my legs to follow each other. I was more than pleased when we reached the village for a rest. There we were shown our billets.

We had to sleep with the cows this time. Walking around I found an empty stable, which was a little consolation. Exhausted, I stretched out on the straw and tried to sleep. I did not sleep well because it was so chilly. Nevertheless, I managed to tough it out that night.

The next day, we were told we would be staying here for ten days. So, finding an old bale house nearby I started a fire. I soon had the fire roaring which was more joyful than anything. I was loafing for now. It has been raining and muddy outside, so the fire feels warm and comfortable.

The name of this village is Bajus. Bajus is very antiquated with its old farmhouses and lanes. The village even has a small schoolhouse and an old-fashioned church. Sunday morning, when they all attend church, is the only time that you see the people looking respectable and well groomed.

The surrounding hills made the village very quaint, as well as the springs running through the fields. Another feature contributing to a countrified look was the clear spring water, cascading down each side of the road.

December 10—I walked with a chum to a town to buy leather. The name of the place is Bruay, a mining town with a population of about fifty thousand people. Girls as well as men worked in the mine pits. It was here in Bruay I had a sizable feed of eggs, chipped potatoes and tea. But before that meal, we went into a store and ate two dozen oysters and some ham. We had a great time. We pranced around the town as though we were the only important ones in town.

It was Sunday again, but the days are all alike in France. Nevertheless, it was a relief being away from the sound of the guns and the buzzing of the shells. About five hundred men joined us during our ten-day lay over in Bajus. Consequently, we were very busy until the last day.

December 20—Leaving Bajus we walked another six miles, reaching another small village called Vernis about midday. It is a real mud hole. Here we had to search for places to sleep, and for a workshop. We are now within three miles of the trenches.

After tramping around, we found a cowshed. We cleaned the place out and built some bunks for sleeping, but it was very chilly. It was as if no roof ever existed. So, we made the best of it in this old place.

Christmas Day was very quiet. For breakfast our food consisted of one slice of bread, a piece of bacon and tea. For dinner we had stew. At supper we had one slice of bread and cheese with tea.

Talk about Christmas Day in the workhouse. They had it all over us poor fellows especially when you read in the papers how the boys in France enjoyed their Christmas dinner. As I said before, you just go along and make the best as possible out of life under the circumstances.

Our men spent time in the trenches at Vimy Ridge. They spent eighteen days in the trenches knee-deep in mud and water. We had thirty men killed and wounded.

The men spent Christmas Day and New Year's Day in the trenches. I can tell you; to them another Christmas in the trenches is out of the question. It was so inhibited, wet and muddy.

On January 8 the men came out of the trenches for a rest at a place called Camblain-L'Abbé. Camblain-L'Abbé was about eight miles from the front line. It was here they would clean up and get ready to go back in about a week.

January 14—The men had to go back to the trenches. Certain ones were cheery, but the majority of them preferred to stay out of the trenches. It was no use feeling dull. It was your duty to go fight in the trenches. You had to make the best of it. The thought of getting leave had made them feel a little better. It was time for our Division to get leave this month.

On January 18, they came out and arrived at their place of rest about 2:30 p.m. They were billeted in huge huts. We went there to see to their boots that were in a very poor state. Many boots had hardly any sole left on them.

The men were glad to get out of the trenches again to have a rest. The stories they told me were unbelievable.

We took a lot of new men in with us this trip, and they were not so eager to go back in the trenches again. The first time it seemed like a circus to them. It was only after getting shot at that they soon had a different opinion.

The men all had coughs owing to the wet and the mud. It was impossible to keep the men's feet dry. Although they got a dry pair of socks every morning, their boots get so saturated that a pair of dry socks remained dry for only a few minutes.

The men had a better rest this time. Usually, when they come out of the trenches, worry was written over their faces. This time they seemed to be more relaxed. So, all of us did take advantage of the short rest. We made the best of it by eating, drinking and having an excellent time. After the rest it was back to the trenches.

January 19—We were back in our cow shed again to settle down for another eight days work getting boots ready for the men by the time they came out of the trenches.

Now we hear a lot of peace talk, and the men are betting on the time and day the war would finish.

Again, for six days Fritz was very quiet, but from behind our lines our guns continued feeding them iron rations. We were busy fixing boots to supply the men with dry ones. Every spare moment we used to slaughter livestock for food.

Our men came out of the reserve trenches for a six-day rest and cleanup. Then, it was back into the line again. We had only four casualties this day. As the battalion was coming out of the trenches, one officer, Lt. Clark of "C" Company, was snipered. The bullet smashed into his chest and out his back. He is now lying in serious condition.

The weather has been terribly cold because of having snow and frost for about two weeks.

The men are now out for another six-day rest. In huts they are coping with this numbing weather. They at least had a jovial time, not having much to do but clean up and relax.

We were paid, and for several days we kept the place lively. While we had the chance, we took advantage of all the food and drink. On the morning of February 7 the men went back to the trenches to do another eighteen days.

February was a quiet time, but we were preparing for a raid, which was pulled off early on the morning of March 1 [1917].

Our battalion suffered heavy losses, at the same time losing our Colonel [Beckett] and Adjutant. Also ten other officers and one hundred fifty men were wounded. Fifty-five men were killed and ninety men were missing.

The men came out for a rest on March 2, and they needed it badly after doing such work. Nevertheless, it was a sad day knowing we had lost so many men.

March 4—Our sadness continued today as we buried the Colonel and the Major who was second in command. The battalion paraded to the cemetery where the band played the Dead March. Then, the firing party fired over their graves, giving them a full military funeral.

Now the men are getting ready for another turn in the trenches. We have new men to fill up the gaps and a new Colonel to take the men into action. After fifteen days of reorganizing two Companies, we were ordered up to the trenches for working parties. The rest of the battalion went to Château de La Hai about three miles from the line. There on a hill in the woods, we were put in tents.

It is now March 19. The wind is blowing, the rain is pouring down, and it kept up until early morning. It was miserable! We were in constant fear that our tent would be swept away. The rain had turned into thickly falling snow when we looked out the next morning. To be in a tent without a fire at this time of year is no cinch. But, we are tough now and think we can stand anything.

It had been dry for a week, and the dust began flying. Now, the mud was flying.

We have to walk about three miles for water, so you can imagine the men not able to wash too many times a day. We stayed here for a week and only two days being dry.

March 26—Monday the men went to the trenches and we came back to the town of Hirsin and were billeted in a house. The family lived in one part of the house, and we were in a tiny room adjacent to theirs. The home was the best place we have had yet as it was comfortable and dry with a stove in the room. Also, we were close to the station and a coal pit.

We were not out of the reach of Fritz's guns because the Huns had already bombed Hirsin with a few shells. But, you talk about mud! The mud was everywhere, so it was a luxury to be in a house once again.

The first night we slept on the floor of the little room allotted us, and it was very comfortable. The next day the French woman said, "No, Bon. There is no excuse for that!" So, she cleaned a room upstairs and made beds for the three of us. She actually put clean sheets on the beds with our blankets. In addition, coffee was made for us several times during the day. They were the best-natured people we had ever met.

We entered the month of April with our guns roaring away. During the last week of March several Huns came over and gave themselves up. One individual wanted to use one of our machine guns on his own trenches. He said they were treated so badly they had only one meal in three days.

A similar occurrence happened at Vimy. Two German officers were saying that the war would end this month. We were hoping the war would end too.

I took a little stroll to the cemetery at La Ville Au Bois. It was here that our old Lt. Colonel Beckett, Major J.M. Langstaff and two of our boys lay side by side. At the head of each grave stood a cross, engraved with the words, Rest in Peace.

With pencil in hand, sometime between the March 1, 1917, trench raid and the battle of Vimy Ridge on April 9, 1917, Bert writes an inspiring poem. The poem is called:

The Boys of the 75th

"What are we fighting for?" the boys will say, Old Fritz, the same will matter. But all the boys of the 75th stand by country and their colours.

We went to Belgium bright and gay, and in those trenches we had to stay. "Up to our waist in mud and clay to do our bit," that's what we say.

We were in this place for just four weeks, and all the trenches were our streets. No side walks there, no asphalt roads, but trench mats, mud and rat hole walls.

From there we tramped it to the Somme, but not so bright and merry, we heard it was a lot worse place, nothing but what the boys could face.

When we arrived at Tarry Hill, the camp for us to rest, it was for us to make a nest to sleep and do our best.

Next day the orders came to move, and then we had to hustle to put our packs into the store and draw our ammunition.

When it was dark the boys moved off, with all their harness on them, the band played in the good old style, and they heard the tune for over a mile.

The mud up there was very thick, but in those trenches we had to stick. The guns each side sent shell for shell, and the boys said it was perfect Hell.

It came our time to charge old Fritz with bombs and rifle and the bayonet fixed. Over the top we had to go, and chance our luck right through the snow.

We made our mark that very day, but the 75th lost men they say. Good they were from rank and file, but we drove them back for nearly a mile.

We finished our task at the Somme that day and all that was left you could hear them say, "we've done our bit through the mud and clay, for King and country in the usual way."

Out we came drenched to the skin, and cared not a bit for anything. We wandered down to Albert town, and there we got to lay down.

Next day we mustered, the roll was called to find out who was missing. Our Colonel that morn was sad and pale, as the roll book told its awful tale.

Our orders were "be ready to move." So we spent the day just cleaning. Each lad to each other his tale would tell about his comrade and others that fell.

The bugle sounded at seven next morn. We started off in a good rainstorm. It was always our luck to start that way, but there wasn't a lad that wanted to stay.

We marched for days through country and town till at last we came to the place set down. A village called Bajus was the name, it was there our boys had to train.

They spent ten days training our men, and waited orders to move again. They came, and off we set from that little place, to see the trenches in the ridge old Fritz to face.

Colonel Beckett would say in his old fashion way, "Men you've done it before, you can do it today." He was proud of his lads for what they had done, he never forgot the deeds at the Somme.

Our time had come for us at the Vimy Ridge, and there to do our duty as other men did. Our casualties started the very first night as we entered the trenches on the right.

There was nothing much done till away in March, then a raid was pulled off one night in the dark.

Old Frtiz seemed to know we were coming just then. He outnumbered our boys again and again.

Some gas was put over, but turned with the wind, the Huns they all knew it and just simply grinned. But the boys they went over and tackled them right, we got in their trenches and made them all fight.

On this occasion we will never forget, all the boys in the outfit will tell you that yet. We lost our Colonel and Major Langstaff, they died like heroes, they fought till the last.

They lay in the graveyard not far from the Ridge, with others beside them that fell as they did. They did their duty that terrible night, we will never forget that month or the fight.

When relieved the next day we came out for a rest, we needed it badly-the biggest and best. Our outfit was crippled, the men badly beat, our clothes were all torn, and kit-that all went.

Our Colonel was gone, some officers too, those that were left said, "what shall we do?" We wanted to keep our boys together and shout "75 now and forever!"

So they found us a Colonel, a jolly good fellow, the right kind of man and not a bit yellow. He said to the boys, "I will see all right, we will soon have the outfit ready to fight."

Just three weeks passed, we were ready again to go to the trenches and fight just the same. We never lost courage, and that you will see, for we have a good leader we all will agree.

> When the war is over and our duty done, we will go back home with the laurels won. Then the people will say of Toronto's own, "here come the boys that are so well known."
>
> Now here's to the land of the Maple Leaf, the place where we long to be. Just three good cheers for the 75th who fought for their King and liberty.
>
> Written by Private H.B. Cooke
>
> 75th Canadians

Our last battle resulted in two officers killed and two officers wounded. Also, numerous men were wounded. Consequently, the boys came out of the trenches for a rest.

We are going to take Vimy Ridge. So, the men go back to the trenches after a six-day rest to prepare for the advance.

On the morning of April 8, our guns started blasting all along the ridge. Almost a thousand guns opened fire. Everything seemed to be on fire in Fritz's line. After the barrage had lifted, we went, engaging everything in front of us.

We gained our objective! We seized the ridge forcing Fritz backwards about two miles. In the process we took nearly four thousand prisoners. Up until noon, our casualties were three officers wounded, and three killed. An additional one hundred fifty men were classified as walking wounded. Also another one of our old 75th officers, Mr. Elliot, was killed. He had been with us all along the line from the beginning.

It was a sight to see the prisoners coming down the line—they looked like poor despicable souls. Prisoners badly wounded were taken to our dressing station before being taken down the line. The French people watched them coming down in batches of several hundreds. They were delighted to see such a vast number. We were all eager to see the news in tomorrow's paper. The victory at Vimy was a feather in the Canadians' cap.

The taking of the famous Vimy Ridge has cost thousands of lives. The French lost terribly at the same place but this time we were prepared to take it and did so with little loss of life. The prisoners say the war would soon be over. They knew they were beaten. Their losses were enormous, and the men looked downtrodden and fed up with the war. They admitted to having no food for days, and looked as if they had not shaved or washed for some time.

Our boys came out for a rest on April 13 after their skillful work. They looked as though they had been battered about too. After a wash and cleanup coupled with a night of rest, they were able to tell a few stories of how and what they did. They would also show each other different equipment taken from Fritz. Certain individuals had revolvers; others had taken money and different paraphernalia, just to remind them of the fighting at Vimy Ridge.

We had lost more of our commanders who had been with us throughout the whole campaign. But their time had come! Several officers joining us a few days before Vimy were also killed or wounded.

Mr. Kappell, another of our old 75th was killed. He had been moved to another unit in February. After our loss March 1, he was recalled to take command of "B" Company again. The day we took the ridge he was killed.

Vimy Ridge will always ring in our ears for many a long day. It was a glorious victory, and it cost us a lot of brave men. Now we have to get organized to move again.

We now have new officers, and additional men are on the way. Then, we will have another task to do. It certainly will not be another Vimy. The Huns are probably still running, and unable to dig themselves in. So, we were all able to have some time now for resting.

We now have a new Colonel. He is a fine fellow coming from the 67th Battalion and is reorganizing the Battalion. Portions of the boys' clothing were stripped to rags from the battle at Vimy.

So, every man was being fitted out with new boots and clothing. He was also giving us half a day for sports activity, which delighted everyone. A little sport is beneficial. Extra sports would be preferred to help us forget the ordeal we have gone through in the past.

Neuville-St. Vaas is the name of the town where we are resting. It is another little old-fashioned village with its old-fashioned farmhouses, and church. Nearly all the houses are beer shops or candy shops. The people here are out to make all the money they can out of us.

Because officers have been scarce, certain individuals of our unit have been made officers this time. Our men have gone through the mill, so they make much better officers than the green officers. They know how to handle the men in the trenches.

April 23—The battalion had a half-day and held some good sports, all kinds of races and games. Another event was having a greasy pig to catch, which caused ample excitement. It was a splendid day and finished up with a ball and football match. All the men enjoyed themselves.

The General and all the officers were present and had an excellent time. We now received orders to move to a camp called Canada Camp the following day. The camp was built in the woods, and it was here a battalion took form. We were to get ready for the front line again.

Every night the weather was ideal for us to play games. We were also having new men arriving. So, in a few days we would be forcing Fritz out of their trenches once more.

May 6—Our battalion was inspected by the General and he inspected all of us. It lasted five hours. At the conclusion he addressed us by saying he was delighted with the battalion. He also said it was the best battalion he had ever inspected.

May 7—Today being Monday we had orders to move to Betheniville Woods. The Colonel gave us all the morning for the sports of baseball and boxing, and the weather was grand. At 2:30 p.m. the men formed up and marched away.

We did get to our camp near the front line. A few tents were already there. Naturally, we had to make our own shelter. With a little determination, we built a shelter and stayed a few days.

On May 9, the boys were ordered to the trenches.

We now came down to Carency to fix up the transports. When our staff arrived, we did have time to rest. As the night came, we had no place to sleep. But we managed to find a tent. At about 8:00 p.m., an officer came along and took away our tent, and we now had the sky for a roof! At some time during the night little drops of water falling on my face woke me. The rain soon ceased, and I finally managed to fall asleep. Altogether I did sleep rather well.

We moved the next morning, pitching our tent up on a hill. We managed to make the tent comfortable, despite having to carry all our gear up the hill. I can tell you we had some time!

It is now Sunday and very hot. So, we did not trouble ourselves making a hut. But, about 9:00 p.m. it started raining and we had to scout around to find some material for making a shelter. By the time we found the material and had the hut erected, the rain had stopped. We were now established with a hut. The place where we are camping is near a French cemetery. It is the cemetery where thousands of our soldiers are buried who died at Vimy Ridge. It is a very mournful sight to see.

On November 17, Brigadier-General Victor Odlum's 11th Brigade took Desire Trench and beyond. Conditions were unbelievably awful. "With the snow and rain," reported General Watson, "the men's clothing becomes so coated with mud, great coat, trousers, puttees and boots sometimes weighing 120 pounds, that many could not carry out relief." On November 21, 1916, General Haig finally called a halt.

By mid November 1916, the Somme offensive had petered out. The British army was marking time in northern France, shivering in the coldest winter in fifty years. By December, the shattered battalions of the Canadian 4th Division, which had fought so hard to capture the Regina Trench, had moved north to join their compatriots.

Change was in the wind! New and powerful personalities were determined to transform the war of attrition into a decisive war of movement. But before the great breakthrough could be achieved, one obstacle had to be eliminated. The Vimy bastion must be captured and held.

Six hundred thousand allied soldiers—including twenty-four thousand young Canadians—had been killed or mutilated on the Somme. Julian Byng was determined that there should be no repetition of that bloodbath, which had seen men with little training and less understanding of battle hurled in dense waves against the German machine guns. The Somme's lessons must be studied and applied to the exercises that would take place behind the Canadian lines.

Arthur Currie, the commanding officer of the 1st Division, shared similar beliefs. He did not accept the excuses given at the Somme. It was said the men were not sufficiently trained for anything more sophisticated. To this alibi Currie had a blunt response: "Take time to train them."

Never before had an Allied attack been planned with such care and common sense.

At army headquarters at Lillers, France, unit officers studied a large-scale Plasticine model of the ridge, which showed with amazing accuracy each small contour and fold in the ground. Behind the lines a full-scale replica of the German defenses on Vimy Ridge was laid out on the ground, marked with white tape and coloured flags. Trenches, roads, machine-gun emplacements and strong points were accurately located from air photographs. Day after day the attacking battalions practiced on this replica until each man knew not only his own task, but also the tasks of those in his immediate vicinity.

Every day, mixing freely with the troops, the quiet friendly figure of the Corps Commander, General Julian Byng, could be seen going over the area with the battalions, explaining details, encouraging, watching, assessing. The Canadians took to Byng. They liked his casual fashion of returning salutes, his humble manner and his obvious common sense. When the troops saw him squatting on the ground, drawing diagrams in the dirt for the officers clustered around him, the soldiers felt a new confidence.

But, any soldier who peered over the Canadian bulwark at the German line on Vimy Ridge must have felt a certain sinking of the heart. The enemy's position was impressively strong.

Nevertheless, the feeling of the Canadian soldier's dominance over the Germans is reinforced by one of Bert's entries. Four days after the battle, on April 13, 1917, Bert wrote that the Huns were probably still on the run and unable to dig themselves in.

Although Bert's role at Vimy was in a back-up capacity, he reveals to us that the individual Canadian soldier felt superior to his German counterpart. It made no difference what function the Canadian soldier performed. It would seem that this collective feeling resulted in the Canadian Corps maintaining leverage in all phases of battle. Victory stemmed from that feeling, a result of the training given by officers and commanders.

Bert's written account of the battle was brief. Nevertheless, he knew the significance of Vimy Ridge, and of the previous defeat the French had experienced. The victory was definitely a feather in the Canadians' cap and a huge accomplishment, despite the heavy loss of life.

Vimy was all Canadian and was the one clear-cut tactical success of the larger battle of Arras. The Canadians were the deliverers of freedom to France and the rest of Western Europe.

In later years, after the slaughter was over and the grass had done its work, Canada put the most graceful of all First World War monuments at the top of Vimy Ridge, and sheep graze now on some of the most richly fertilized terrain in human history.

Now a reorganized 75th Battalion begins moving north toward Lens. They were to penetrate deep into the German lines south of Lens to replace the British Corps. They now looked across at Lens and at two hills, Sallaumines and Hill 70, that flanked the city.

With new commanders and replacement troops, the capture of Lens and Hill 70 would be a frightening task. Would they be able to handle the house-to-house fighting and hand-to-hand combat that was to come?

Brigadier General Victor W. Odlum, CO of 11th Brigade of 4th Division under Major-General David Watson. Odlum was the chief exponent of the trench raid. (The John A. Hertel Co. Ltd., Toronto, 1919)

Major-General David Watson, commanding officer of the 4th Canadian Division. (The John A. Hertel Co. Ltd., Toronto, 1919)

Major-General Arthur W. Currie, 1st Canadian Division Commanding Officer. (The John A. Hertel Co. Ltd., Toronto, 1919)

Lieutenant General Sir Julian Byng, British officer who took over the Canadian Corps from Lieutenant General Sir Edwin Alderson. (The John A. Hertel Co. Ltd., Toronto, 1919)

Commanding officer of the 3rd Army, General Sir Edmund Allenby. (The John A. Hertel Co. Ltd., Toronto, 1919)

The cemetery at La Ville au Bois, France. (Milly Walsh)

CHAPTER 7

Bullets and Billets

When I got over here I began to realize there was a war on and the rumble of the guns doesn't give you a chance to forget it either, but I guess the only thing is to keep my heart up and my head down.

Private Henry Orde, rifle grenade operator, 90th Winnipeg Rifles,
144th Battalion. Killed in action August 15, 1917, on first day of
battle of Hill 70, Lens, France, aged eighteen.

I left for England May 21 for ten days on leave. While on leave, I got sick and had to stay in bed two days. Consequently, I was admitted into the hospital for three days.

I started back to France June 4 from Cirencester and stayed in London for the night. I then went on to Folkestone on the 5th. When I arrived, I was put into a rest camp. It was here I rested for three hours.

I was marched off to the ship after having dinner and then sailed for Boulogne. We were then rushed off up the hill to a rest camp. We were told that breakfast would be served at one o'clock in the morning. Also, we were to be ready to go to the station at 1:30 a.m. We marched off to the station entrance at 3:00 a.m. but didn't start out until four o'clock in the morning. I arrived at Bethune at midday after having dinner. I then set off for camp and arrived at six o'clock in the evening, finding all my pals in commendable form.

Our boys went into the trenches on June 5 and are expecting to go over the top on the night of June 8.

Our guns started blasting, and it seemed like an earthquake. They riddled old Fritz's lines for a few hours. Then, about 12:00 p.m., our boys made a raid on his trenches. They were able to do a tremendous amount of damage. We had light casualties with only nine killed and a small number slightly wounded. Several of our boys were new men. It was a critical experience for them because it was their first time in the battle line.

The men came out of the trenches for a rest in the woods. After resting for eight days we then returned to another camp near Vimy Ridge. We worked a few days here at Vimy before going out for the divisional rest. Also, we had several more men coming into the battalion. We would then be up to full strength.

June 28—We have now been out of the trenches for three weeks. So, every afternoon we participated in sports activities. Today we had sad news. One of our scouts blew his brains out last night. He was a fine fellow, and no one would have thought he would have done such a thing. But this life is enough to make a fellow do anything. We are going in to the trenches tomorrow for four days. After the four days we go out for a divisional rest.

June 29—We received news that the first American contingent had arrived in France. Plenty of room exists for them, and we hoped they would accomplish as much as the Canadians have. Rain had been falling all day and it was muddy again up to our necks. It is wretched for the cooks as they have to prepare the meals in the open. Consequently, they had troubles keeping the fires going.

We expected to go back into the trenches. The boys were all ready to go, but the order was cancelled with another order. We were to be ready to move in two days. The move was better for the boys than the trenches.

Yesterday we saw lots of prisoners coming from the trenches. This exodus of prisoners was the result of the previous night's advance, which was very successful. Our boys put up a heavy bombardment upon receiving word that our artillery was strong.

The last few days the weather has been against us. Nevertheless, it was delightful for the crops that were looking very healthy.

July 1—We set off for a village called Estrée-Cauchie. For a tiny village, it was located in a pleasant spot. It was here we rested for a month. We were staying in barns and huts and had a pleasant hut for work. Also, we slept out in fields with the corn and orchards all around us. We had an exceptional view of the country for miles. It was admirable to see the women and girls working the land and doing all the farm work. Occasionally you would see an old man among them. The whole vegetable line looked immaculate, and an excellent crop expected.

We have a fine battalion now with lots of new men. So, now we are up to full strength. All the men had time to wash and shine their kits. You would think the battalion had just reached the country.

They got plenty of training, rising in the morning at 4:30 a.m. Coffee was served at 5:00 a.m., and then we participated in physical training until 7:30 a.m. We then had breakfast after which we had special training until 12:30 p.m. We got the afternoon off for sports such as football and baseball.

July 10—His Majesty King George V came, so we lined the streets to give him a cheer. He looked splendid.

July 13—It was a hot, blistering day. We had a nine-mile brigade march starting out at ten o'clock in the morning, and we did not return until 3:00 p.m. that afternoon. The march was with full transport and entirely in full marching order. The march was very strenuous, and several men fell out before we reached our camp. I was weak from fatigue myself. So, when I got back to the hut I just dropped my kit and was pleased to lie down for a rest for part of the day. My feet and shoulders were terribly sore.

In the evening a football match was played between the details and "C" Company. It was relaxing to sit down and watch the game, "C" Company winning by a score of 1 to 0. It was a very exciting time.

We had a decent, dry canteen to buy drinks, but our money soon disappeared as we had only fifteen francs pay. We were expecting double pay in a day or two; then the boys would be able to have a favourable time. That day eventually came. During our stay the majority of us spent our pay by patronizing the high spots nearly every night.

The best platoon in the battalion is getting a prize of two thousand francs from the Colonel. I can tell you the men worked on their kits and clothes nearly all night.

The time came for inspection. The contest was keen with thirteen platoons winning. Now they have to compete for the divisional prize, which was work. The winning platoon gets to go to Paris for five days. Every man was trying their utmost, and I thought each platoon would stand a chance.

The day of July 20 was lovely, and everything was in order. So the division decided to set aside the day for sports. Every battalion was represented, and several boys of our battalion won prizes. I did feel they had a chance to win.

On July 21, the General inspected all the transports of the 11th Brigade. All the equipment was loaded, taken to a field and unloaded for inspection. It was all accomplished in full marching order.

The inspection took all day, and it was not until six o'clock in the evening when we finished. You cannot imagine the relief we experienced. We wandered back to camp and had an excellent supper waiting for us.

On July 23 the platoon competition took place. Thirteen platoons won in fine style. Every man was in top form with shiny knockers. Nothing could beat them.

In the evening, I went to a banquet and had a grand time. Wine, beer, and fruit were served in abundance, and a concert was given by the men.

We were inoculated the next day. The inoculation left most of the men feeling sickly, so we were given forty-eight hours to get over the effect.

It was a warm day but pleasant enough for walking. So I took a walk for a few miles to a likable little town called Aubigny. I arrived at noon. I sat down in a French restaurant for a meal, took a little walk around the town and strolled back to camp. I arrived just in time for supper.

Now the men are getting ready to go back into the trenches. On July 26 they moved off after walking a few miles. After supper we moved on into the support trenches.

We stayed in Carency. As usual, we had to salvage all the material to build a shack. Before nightfall we had an admirable place with beds for sleeping.

The platoon winning the contest was kept out of the line until they had completed their leave to Paris. This gesture was part of the prize.

On July 29 we had one officer killed and one private. Fritz has a new gun now, which he used to fire at our observation balloons.

Every night the Germans would send over a few shells. Although the shells exploded with gusto, the German gunners had difficulty getting the range.

Our men were in cellars in a huge town called Liévin. We had driven the Germans out of this town, and it was away from that gigantic gun.

It is a shame to see the furniture left in the houses by the French. When they were forced out by the Germans, all kinds of household goods were left. A number of the men even had a piano in the cellar.

We now proceeded to the front line near Lens, which we hoped to capture soon. At the time the weather was against us, with rain and mud up to our necks. Making a fire for some warmth is delightful because it has been raining for eight days.

On August 11 the boys came out for a three-day rest as far as Vimy Ridge. We were very lucky because only a few were killed and wounded. Two officers were among the wounded.

On the night of August 15 they moved up the line again into a part of Lens that was captured.

On the morning of August 16, at eight o'clock, they had to go over the top and capture some more of the town. Quarter Master Cuthbert was killed at that exact moment. A German shell plunged on him as he sat by the entrance of a dugout.

His death was a shock to us because it was his first trip to the line. We had lost a good pal. He will be remembered by all, because he was one of the few old boys who were left. Also, several others were killed. It was a sad trip. Old Fritz always seemed to know where we were going over with massed troops and machine guns. It is arduous fighting from house to house.

Tonight, August 17, we were being relieved of duty and came back a few nights to reorganize. We will miss our old pals that have gone.

August 27 was an interesting day. A German plane dropped from the clouds this afternoon. The pilot made a dive for one of our observation balloons. As he made his dive he managed to set it on fire. On his return one of our scout planes tackled him but was rather slow for him, so the German plane sped skillfully off into the evening.

The German plane came again. The pilot dove for another balloon and struck it with another firebomb. Our aircraft was waiting this time. They put a barrage in front of him so that he could not escape. Thirty of our planes seemed to drop from the clouds and tackled him—one was above the German and riddled him with bullets making him plummet to the ground. It was a momentous sight.

Soon thousands of soldiers were at the crash scene. One of Fritz's soldiers was taken prisoner, and the other soldier was dead. The German soldier said the plane was one of their latest models, and the only plane like it in Germany.

We came out on the night of August 27 and walked to Gouy-Servins. This time we had very few casualties with only two wounded and two killed. We then came back to the ridge for eight days before another eight days of fighting. We billeted in a château with a few men put in barns and stables.

On August 29 we were holding Corps sports, and the men of our Battalion are in fine shape. Thousands of men were there and all the Canadian Generals. It was some exciting sport. Our special platoon and snipers did well in the competition, taking two firsts and two seconds and the shield. Also, each man had from one to three medals. We had six lads entered. Four of them won the laurels, and nothing could beat them. The special race of the day was the relay, and the General said it was the best he had seen. Our boys won it. The weather had been cooperative, and it was a lovely day.

On September 1, we came out to Liévin, staying here a few days. During our stay we lived in dugouts built by Fritz.

The Germans were shelling this place very heavily. But we outgunned them five to one. Liévin was once a fine town, but now it is in ruins. Fritz had dug himself in and made bomb-proof cellars for protection.

The night of September 3, Fritz started to shell Liévin at 1:45 a.m. and sent thousands of gas shells. He pounded for nearly two hours. I will never forget it as I had my gas helmet on for one and three-quarter hours. A number of our boys inhaled a little gas but nothing of a serious nature.

For the Fifth Divisional Artillery, it was a surprise because it was their first taste of battle. Close to where I was standing four horses were killed. The four riders were also wounded. The next night we came out and journeyed to Servins for three days to reorganize.

For four days our boys were training for a battle. On October 2, a single soldier out of the 102 men took a mad fit, loaded his rifle and shot two officers. One of the officers was Major Bull of the 75th. He took a bullet through the neck, although it was not fatal. That same bullet went through the breast and out of the back of Staff Captain Martin. It was a horrendous wound. He was lucky to survive.

On the morning of October 3, we had a rush order to move out back from the line to Estrée-Souchez. On October 4 we were going still farther back. We did not know where we were going or why. At noon on October 5, we started a steady march of six miles to Houdain. We arrived at 3:30 p.m. and got into billets. It was a pleasant little place, and we all had a friendly time feeding on ices and chips.

The few days we were here we had a good time. We attended relaxing night concerts too.

The morning of October 11, we had breakfast at 4:45 a.m. and fell in formation at 7:30 a.m. to entrain for an unknown place. We were all in boxcars waiting to depart. It was a fine day but terribly cold. We started off at 9:30 a.m. arriving at a point at 1:30 p.m.

We reached a little village called Wittes after a march of about twelve miles. There we had a job to find billets. I slept in a pig sty with lots of strays. Some calves in the next sty kept me company. I did not need anyone to rock me to sleep. So, I just dropped off to sleep and slept till noon.

We had no orders for the next day. Nevertheless, we were called at six o'clock in the morning when breakfast was served. Our day's rations were also issued for another march.

We fell into formation at 7:30 a.m. It was a wet morning, and we had to wear our rubber sheets. The rain stopped and the sky cleared after we had been on the road for about half an hour.

We stopped for dinner at 12:30 p.m. We happened to be near a house so I went in and bought a mess tin of coffee and some bread and butter. After a one-hour rest we moved on again and reached our destination, Saint-Marie-Kerque. We marched about ten miles, but it seemed like twenty miles.

We were put in a barn with lots of straw. The farmer here had been a soldier from Flanders and was very fluent at speaking English. So, we went into the farmhouse and bought eggs and coffee. We were even able to get warm by the fire. At the time of the retreat he said he had had no food for four days. But he was discharged so he could care for a family of six boys at home. It was refreshing to find a Frenchman who could speak English.

We were now reaching Flanders again, and the people spoke a mixture of Flemish and French. Portions of them spoke a little English. We had supper about 7:00 p.m.which consisted of tea, dates, hard tack and cheese. We then retired for the night.

In the morning we awoke about 7:30 a.m. and went for a well-prepared breakfast. We expected to be moving again. But, we were delighted to know the day was for resting. The news pleased us all.

The next morning started out fine. Then, about eight o'clock the rain commenced, making it terribly chilly. So, we went into the farmhouse and sat around the fire chatting. We were also able to have a shave, wash and a general cleanup.

It was still raining, so after supper the Flying Corps put on a picture show for us. They had a fine camp here. I went over and looked around and saw many fine flying machines. At seven o'clock we gathered around the small picture house of the RFC. When the doors opened, men came rushing in out of the pelting rain. I just managed to get in.

It was a commendable show. Charlie Chaplin starred in *The Perfect Lady*, and the movie did cheer us up.

The worst was yet to come. Upon leaving the show, we went out into a night that was pitch-black and pouring rain. We had a mile walk to get back to camp. I can tell you we were plastered from head to foot with mud and soaked to the skin with rain. It is not pleasant getting up in the morning and having to put on your wet pants. But, a shining sun gave us a chance to get dry. I was hoping the sun would last.

The weather cleared the next day, and it was a relief to get fresh air.

Because it was Sunday, our battalion held a church parade in the morning. So we all had the remainder of the day to rest.

The boys took advantage of the fine day roaming various fields picking berries and visiting orchards. The men waited for chances to pick pears or apples from the trees. It was amusing watching their antics.

The next morning was fine. In the afternoon a football match was played. The match was between the 75th and 102nd, and the game ended in a draw. Our band played near the village church, and the old priest was delighted. He asked them to play the "Marseillaise" and the "Canadian Air" that the priest enjoyed. Our boys were paid which pleased them more.

In the evening the boys had a friendly time drinking which helped them to forget their troubles.

The next day the men were busy on drill and repairing their boots. A football match was played in the afternoon that they all enjoyed.

Major-General Arthur Currie returned to his new command. His task under Sir Henry Horne's First Army was to restrain the German division that might otherwise stop Haig's Flanders offensive. Haig had ordered that attackers must control any ground they took. To Currie that meant exposing troops to needless casualties. His Canadians would raid, destroy and return to their trenches before the Huns could catch them.

In a series of carefully planned raids, Currie showed how to hit without getting badly hurt. On June 8, nine brigades from the 3rd and 4th divisions penetrated deep into the German lines south of Lens. The efforts paid off, despite

100 killed and 709 casualties. Two weeks later the Germans pulled back to Avion fully aware that their position was now hopelessly weakened.

By this time the Canadian Corps had replaced a British Corps in trenches that looked across at Lens and at the two hills, Sallaumines and Hill 70, that flanked the city.

Hill 70 was a bald knob of limestone that the British had taken and lost in 1915 at the battle of Loos. Clumps of miners' cottages on the slopes of the hill provided the Germans a perfect covered approach for their counterattacks. The shell-battered ruins with a maze of cellars, trenches, and tunnels would now be better cover. Machine-gun companies would follow the assault waves. Then they would dig into the hard chalk surface and wait for the counterattacks. Allied artillery, exceeding anything the British had had in 1915, would be waiting for the Huns in a killing ground of the Allies' choosing, not the Germans.

Hill 70 would not be easy. The batteries of British guns available at Vimy had been moved north to Flanders. Many of the remaining guns in the heavy artillery were worn out and no longer accurate.

The Huns had introduced frightening new weapons in July— Flammenwerfers or flamethrowers that threw a jet of fire fifty feet or more. The other cruel weapon was mustard gas. The gas raised agonizing blisters wherever droplets fell, especially wherever the skin was damp.

The weather was miserable at Lens, much as in Flanders and rain washed out Allied Commanders' deadlines.

At dawn on 15 August, ten Canadian battalions scaled their trenches and walked into the barrage. Hill 70 erupted in explosions of flame and dirt in front of them. The Huns, alarmed at the Canadian threat, had sent troops forward, but a diversionary attack by Watson's 4th Division on Lens distracted them. Thick black smoke from five hundred blazing oil barrels spread as a screen over Hill 70. Despite the blinding smoke screen, the German machine-guns spat out five hundred rounds a minute to kill and wound. Within twenty minutes the surviving Canadians were on top of Hill 70. Battalions from the 2nd Division wheeled south, into the mining villages on the slopes, while

Macdonell's 1st Division pushed east and north (after the battle of Vimy Ridge, Macdonell had replaced Currie as commander of the 1st Division). On the far side, Brigadier General F.O.W. Loomis's 2nd Brigade faced a huge chalk quarry and German defenders unshaken by the bombardment. British Columbians and Winnipegers of the 7th and 8th battalions fought from shell-hole to shell-hole, but it was early on August 16 before they were in position. Most men of the battalions were dead or wounded.

As early as 9:00 a.m. on 15 August, the Canadians fought their first counterattack. Attacks kept coming. In the intervals, infantrymen and machine-gunners hacked holes for themselves and their guns, or they cared for wounded comrades. Artillery observers used wireless communication for the first time to zero in on advancing German columns. Long-range artillery shells met the Huns as they marched. German mustard gas shells cost two artillery brigades 178 casualties after gunners had yanked off their masks to see what they were doing. Somehow, the survivors kept the batteries firing.

Hundreds of Germans got through the storm of shrapnel and high explosives and hurled themselves forward with grenades, rifles and the horrifying flamethrowers. Canadians fought back, sometimes hand to hand. In all, the Canadians won five Victoria Crosses at Hill 70.

At dawn on August 18, the Canadians stopped the twenty-first and last German counterattack. The battle for Hill 70 was over. Three of the northwestern suburbs of Lens were in Allied hands. Taking the Hill cost the Canadians 3,527 men. Holding the Hill cost 2,316 more lives. That amount included the hundreds of gunners who had suffered from the Germans' mustard gas. Currie's tactics had paid off; five German divisions had been thrown into the battle at a cost of 20,000 men. For Currie it was the hardest battle in which the Corps had participated. Years later he remembered it as his proudest. The Canadians had cost the enemy far more than they had paid.

Hill 70 did not end the fighting for Lens. Currie ordered a fresh attack before the day ended to clear Germans from more of the mining villages on the slope.

The Allies were only able to half encircle Lens. The reason was that another part of the battle line called for the presence of the Canadian Corps.

Lens had been a tough nut to crack by frontal attack, so the Canadians applied the pincers with flanking assaults.

The 75th had been banged up since the March 1 raid at Vimy Ridge, so the battalion kept being replenished with new men to help in the attempt to capture Lens. But it was a sad campaign for the 75th. The pressure of trench warfare and heavy house-to-house fighting began to take its toll on the battalion and individually.

Spying remained a problem. The Germans always seemed to know when the Canadians were going over the top en masse with machine guns. Anger and resentment added the spark to a soldier's emotional fuse when German shells took the life of comrades. Suicides and soldiers shooting their own officers were grim realities.

The 75th was involved in two of the assaults on Lens. The emotional pressure raised its ugly head with more suicides and isolated cases of men shooting their own officers! As a result of the turmoil, the 75th could only endure four to five days of fighting before going out for a divisional rest. Then they would have to be relieved by another battalion, plus continual replenishing of their own losses.

Over a period of six weeks the 75th played an important role defending various parts of the front line between Lens and Liévin. Their modest back-up role contributed to the overall regression of German troop movement.

Lens stayed under German control, and the Canadian Corps headed into an even uglier, more encompassing tragedy.

For Bert a more personal, clandestine role would soon begin. His own adventures were just beginning.

A switchback railway. Folkstone, England. (Milly Walsh)

King George V. (The John A. Hertel Co. Ltd., Toronto, 1919)

Brigadier General A.C. Macdonnell, 7th Brigade Commander. (The John A. Hertel Co. Ltd., Toronto, 1919)

Main Street in Liévin, France. (Milly Walsh)

CHAPTER 8

Encounters

They died in Hell, they called it Passchendaele.

Siegfried Sassoon, English poet and author,
third Battle of Ypres

On October I started on a sixteen-day leave to England. At 5:00 a.m. it was some walk to the station because it was about five miles. I was supposed to get on the train at Hazebrouck at one o'clock, but did not start until 5:00 p.m. in the evening.

After a weary trip we arrived at Boulogne at 1:30 a.m. We should have been there at 8:00 p.m. We stayed here in Boulogne until 8:00 a.m. which was the morning of October 19. After boarding the boat, I had a pleasant passage over to England and arrived in London at 3:30 p.m. From there I sent a telegram home. After doing a little business in London, I went on to Paddington to catch the train at 6:00 p.m. I arrived at Cirencester at 8:30 p.m. that night.

It was uplifting to meet Auguster, Morris and Harold at the station. We did not have far to walk, and we were soon home. I had a refreshing bath and clean clothing. I was contented to retire for the night after having a filling supper and chat with the family.

I spent a relaxing ten days at home and helped Auguster and the boys pack as they prepared to go back to Canada.

My time was up on Sunday night, October 28. I made the most of my trip and did not start my return until 11:30 p.m. I caught the mail train to London and arrived in London at 4:00 a.m. on October 29. I had forty winks and then started for Folkestone.

I took the boat to Boulogne at 6:30 a. m. I arrived in Boulogne at midday. Upon arriving at the campsite on the hill I was told to go to a different hut. We had dinner at 1:00 p.m., then tea at 4:30 p.m. At 5:30 p.m. we were served with tea and rations for the journey. Then at 10:00 p.m. we fell into formation to go to the station. We were dismissed because the Huns' planes were hovering over us. The Germans were dropping bombs on Boulogne, and we scurried to get under cover. At 11:30 p.m. my group was summoned again, and we were taken to the station. We were bundled into the train and pulled out about 1:00 a.m.

After a chilly ride we arrived at Poperinghe, Flanders, at midday. We then went into town and had dinner. With dinner finished we proceeded to find out the location of our unit. After walking about ten miles, we found them in a place called Brandhoek. After two days back, the boys proceeded up the line to defend it for two days. I was sent to the Brigade School to do training, which was better than the breaches.

For two nights now, Fritz has been flying over in droves. They are dropping bombs all over the area. It got our wind up as we were only in a tent and not protected at all. It was only by providence that we lived through the bombardment. I think I was never so faithful in prayer to God as I was those last two nights. It made one consider that the Almighty is taking care of you.

Our boys were being relieved of duty November 2 and November 3. We now pulled out for another unknown destination. We entrained at Ypres and left for Handzame where we billeted in barns. It was a relief to get out of the mud and away from the roar of the guns. We stayed here for a rest but for how many days we don't know.

The first day was spent cleaning up our gear. The next day was inspection by the General. He said he was pleased the division had done such exemplary work on the front. In addition, he said if other divisions do their part, we would not have to go back to the trenches. However, in the evening a wire came for a battalion to go back to the front line. So, the 75th had to go for three days.

Another draft of 110 men came during those three days. They were staying at the brigade school until the battalion came back. However, they were to be divided into companies. It was grand to see the new men come. But the questions these men asked were funny. They did not like sleeping in barns and cowsheds.

A few men did wind up sleeping in cowsheds next to the cows. The smell was appalling. But an exhausted soldier doesn't worry about the odour when straw is available for sleeping.

We left again for Boulogne on November 9, getting on the train at Caëstre at 2:45 p.m. We arrived at Brandhoek at 4:30 p.m. Here we were put into tents. We started to get some supper by making our own tea, and then we were served with bread, cheese and pickles.

The next morning, we received orders to move up to a camp beyond Ypres. We are to be ready to go to the front line again on November 12.

The area here is some hot shop! We are up to our eyes in mud. A portion of the boys slept in tents, others under old ruins and some under anything for shelter.

Our guns are pounding away night and day, and Fritz is really sending over some heavy stuff. Also, his planes made several bombings during the night and early morning.

It is raining nearly all the time. Because of the pounding of the guns and the shells bursting it is impossible to sleep. Because of being wet and cold, it is difficult to get any kind of rest.

The afternoon of the 12th, the men went into the line again for another four-day spell. In the morning, about breakfast time, a German plane dropped a bomb near our kitchen. One man was killed and six wounded. Also, about fifty men were sent to hospital. They were gassed during a three-day working party.

On November 19, we were relieved of duty after being in the front line for two days. We then pulled out to a place called Watou near Poperinghe. There we had a change of clothing and a bath.

On November 21, we pulled out at eight o'clock in the morning. After walking about two miles we transferred to buses. We then had a three-hour ride to a town called Neuf-Berquin.

We arrived at Neuf-Berquin about 2:30 in the afternoon. We purchased some canned goods and bread from a store, took it into a house and had coffee. We billeted in a school and spent the rest of our time relaxing and eating. The people were very hospitable.

The next morning we fell into formation at 9:30 a.m. We then walked about ten miles to a place called La Bassée. We arrived there about four o'clock, and we were all exhausted. We went to bed after a supper of rabbit stew and tea.

The next morning we fell into formation again, with the weather favorable for marching. A twelve-mile journey sent us through some fair-sized towns. We halted at 11:30 a.m. for dinner. Tea was served with bread, cheese and jam. After a decent rest we started our march again.

After a long walk we arrived at our destination. It was a long time before we could get a billet. After a lot of talk, they put us in a room in the school. We took a walk around Camblain-Châtelain, and it was time for supper, which consisted of stew and coffee.

We are having an excellent time, despite the low morale of the people. We drew our Christmas pay, and several of the men are having a grand time getting drunk every night. The barrooms are well attended every night because the organ is the main attraction. The people put a penny in the slot and away goes the music. The bar maids and soldiers dance together, making everyone seem content. After a lengthy rest of twenty-five days in this place we had orders to move.

So, on December 18 we started off at 8:30 a.m. and arrived at the Château de la Haie at 3:00 p.m.

I had learned that my two brothers Arthur and Walter were nearby, so I set out to find them. Upon finding them, we had a long chat over supper.

The next day at 10:00 a.m. we moved to Neuville-Saint-Vaast. We had dugouts here, so we had to light stoves to keep warm. My platoon has a satisfactory billet at a farmhouse. The people here cleaned the bake house for us, and it made a fine workshop. At night we sat around the fire soaking up the heat, sometimes with a cup of coffee. It was a lot better than sitting in a dugout.

The boys went into the front line December 21, and would be there for twenty-six days. The weather was terribly frigid, and it was difficult obtaining wood to burn. We had to sneak around places and other dugouts to find fuel.

On Christmas Eve the boys had some time in the trenches, with lots to eat and drink. Christmas Day was extra special with beer, rum and roast pork with sauce. Also, there were fried potatoes, Christmas pudding, cigarettes, cigars and a Christmas stocking. I can tell you we had some time. Last year we had nothing under another Colonel.

The line we were in was satisfactory, being huge dugouts. I helped the butcher cut up the meat, and I helped myself to a tasty little morsel every day and cooked it in the dugout.

We had an exceptional time compared with this time last year after being in the front line for thirty days. The boys came back about ten miles from the line and stayed in huts for five days. Each night during that time, they were sent up the front line in working parties. It rained nearly every night and the mud was fierce.

After five days of rain we moved up to Liévin. After staying here for an additional five days, it was back to the front line. We considered ourselves very lucky with only one man killed, and two men wounded.

From the front line we moved out to Servins for ten days of rest, and the boys had a decent time. After our rest of ten days we relocated to Vimy for five days. From here the boys went up to Liévin as working parties. Then, we migrated back to Château de la Haie for another five days.

From Château de la Haie, we withdrew to Camblain-Châtelain for another rest. The people welcomed us here as though the town was our home. They thought a lot of our battalion. Consequently, when we arrived, the men were out looking for beds in private homes. It was refreshing to be in a bed.

The weather was grand for the month, and the first night in the village was lots of fun and music.

This time our stay at this place has not been so pleasant. It has been all work and no play. The men had been worried to death of having to clean and shine up for inspections. They were first inspected by the

Corps Commander and he found many faults. This meant cleaning every little item right down to shining the ammunition.

On February 28, a review was conducted by Sir Douglas Haig himself. He is Commander in Chief of the entire British Forces here in France and Belgium. He is going to inspect our brigade. To make matters worse, we had to march about five miles from the camp to the field. We then stood at parade rest for three hours before the review.

It is miserable having to wear our harnesses for eight hours at a stretch. Instead of men on active service, a person would have thought that the battalion had fallen from a Christmas tree.

We received a lot of praise at the review. Sir Douglas Haig said every man looked admirable and was more than pleased with the steadiness of the men.

We are being transferred on March 3, so I hope the next few days would be a little better.

We left Camblain-Châtelain on Sunday, March 3, at 9:30 a.m. for Hersin. We would be working out of Hersin for ten days as working parties. It was very chilly with drizzling rain making it miserable for walking. At noon we halted for lunch. Tea was served, including bully beef. After a brief rest, we resumed our march. We arrived at our destination exhausted and wet at about 8:00 p.m.

The next day, I paid a visit to a family who had housed me last year. The people were delighted to see me. So, they asked me to sleep there during our stay in Hersin. I can tell you it was a delight to sleep in an actual bed.

On the night of March 9 two commanders stayed with me in the house. The woman had gone to Paris to fetch her daughter home, and the old man was left with the family.

My mates were out for a good time. So, they bought wine, beer and a bottle of whiskey. Despite all the drinking, the old Frenchman started frying steak and potatoes for supper. He and his son were getting pretty drunk and very wobbly. So, I had to finish cooking the supper.

I had a hell of a time there with three crying children and their sick father. I had to put him to bed. I then fed the children and put them to bed too. I even had to lock up the house before retiring myself.

The son forgot to go to work the next morning. He was supposed to leave at 4:00 a.m. but was still too sick. The old man woke up still sick but soon got out of bed. I tell you I had some pandemonium.

On March 11, we left for the line and started from Hersin at three o'clock by transport. After a two-hour ride, we stopped for a rest and were served tea. We then went on our way reaching Liévin at 9:30 p.m. Being the reserve unit, we had a rewarding day.

Fritz was shelling Liévin constantly. So, it was best to keep under cover as much as possible. Consequently, we had fun playing cards and writing letters. After ten days in the line, we came out for five days.

Unknown destinations remained common for Bert and his comrades. It was upon reaching their destinations that they learned where they were. Bert does not mention whether any frustration ever existed over the idea of not knowing a destination.

The 75th continued to fulfill its role as a reserve unit. Nevertheless, as the 75th and the rest of the Corps moved back into the Ypres salient from Lens, that uglier and more encompassing tragedy was Passchendaele. In the Great War, the Canadian Corps, of which the 75th was an integral part, proved itself to be equal of the best troops of the British or French armies. To say more than this would be to state the impossible. To say Bert's exploits were over would be too presumptuous.

In the autumn of 1917 the British had begun a series of operations in the Ypres salient designed to widen the salient. A salient was that part of a trench or fortification that projected towards the enemy. But a series of attacks stuck fast with the coming of the autumn rains. It was highly desirable that the Germans be ejected from the higher ground surrounding Passchendaele before the arrival of the winter. For this purpose it was decided to move in fresh troops. The troops selected were the Canadians; therefore, in October the Corps moved north from Lens to its old fighting ground in the Ypres salient.

On October 26, the Canadians attacked toward Passchendaele Ridge, in conjunction with British troops. Battlefield conditions were horrific. Soldiers trudged forward through mud that was waist-deep. By nightfall the Canadians were in possession of practically all their objectives. Now they were within striking distance of Passchendaele. An attack on October 30 carried them to the outskirts of

Passchendaele, and on November 6 they captured the village, together with the high ground to the northwest. A final assault on November 10 placed in their hands the last remaining spurs of the ridge.

The combat at Passchendaele was of unexampled stubbornness. The German defenses were invulnerable except under the heaviest shellfire, because they were strengthened by numerous concrete "pill-boxes." The machine-gun fire from the pill-boxes was so hot that it was necessary to order a temporary retirement and to reorganize the attack.

The Germans counterattacked at every stage of the operations. The final result, however, was that the Canadians accomplished the task set before them—at the expense of sixteen thousand killed or wounded. Sir Douglas Haig reported that for the second time within the year, Canadian troops had achieved a record of uninterrupted success.

The Canadian Corps returned to the Lens sector after the capture of Passchendaele, where they spent the winter either in rest or holding the line. No further attempt was made at this juncture to capture Lens. Also, the arrival of German reinforcements from the Eastern Front gave the Huns a hold upon Lens, which would have been reckless to dispute. The Canadians had done their full share of fighting during 1917, and after their strenuous efforts at Passchendaele they needed time for rest and recuperation.

Nineteen-seventeen was a year of significant change in the command of the Canadian Corps. Up to and including the battle of Vimy Ridge the command of the Corps had been in the hands of an Imperial officer. In the summer of 1917, however, Sir Julian Byng was promoted to the command of the Third Army. Major-General (now Lieutenant-General) Sir A.W. Currie was appointed as Corps Commander and the Commander of the First Division. General Currie was an officer who rose from the ranks of the Canadian militia. In private life he was a Vancouver businessman interested in real estate and insurance. Therefore, he fittingly typified the civilian character of Canada's army. Under him the Canadian Corps was to achieve its crowning success of the year 1918.

The big push was now on. The movement and positioning of German and Allied forces was indicative of another clash in the spring of 1918. The Canadian Corps would be the spearhead.

Ypres, Belgium. Butter Street before and after the bombardment. (Milly Walsh)

Ypres, Belgium. The Merghelynck's Museum before and after the bombardment. (Milly Walsh)

Station Street in Ypres was bombarded during the 1914-1915 campaign. (Milly Walsh)

75th Battalion headquarters in Liévin, France. (Milly Walsh)

Sir Douglas Haig, Commander in Chief of the British Forces in France and Belgium. (The John A. Hertel Co. Ltd., Toronto, 1919)

CHAPTER 9

The Night March

There's a little wet home in the trench,

That the rain storms continually drench.

A dead cow close by,

with her hooves in the sky,

and she gives off a beautiful stench.

Underneath us, in place of a floor,

is a mess of cold mud and some straw,

and the Jack Johnsons roar as they speed through the air,

O'er my little wet home in the trench.

"Canadian Song." Reprinted from The Beaver,
October/November 1989, p. 28.

France—1918 Spring Offensive, March 21, 1918

On March 21 the order came to advance. We received news that the Germans had advanced, and clashes with them had been lively for days. We shifted around, not settling in any place as the troops were being manoeuvred around ready to burst in at any place at a minute's notice.

About March 29, we held the line for ten days in front of Rocklincourt. We had a rather profitable time here. In the evacuated trenches our boys salvaged the contents of cigarettes and several other pieces of paraphernalia. Another store with new clothes was also seized.

After our stay in Rocklincourt we came out to Euchree Camp near Arras. We were only here for part of that day. Then, for one night we had to go back on the left flank to reline the CMR [*Canadian Mounted Rifles*]. We left the CMR to take our position for six days the following night. Then, we returned, taking on the role of reserves for two or three days. The weather was chilly. Despite having snow on April 19 we had sturdy cellars to stay in at Petit Vimy.

On April 23 we moved up to the front line. As we moved up the hill, I fell over some of Fritz's barbed wire, and a barb penetrated my knee. Before nightfall I was taken to the dressing station. I wound up in bed for three days here at the station not fit to walk. When the three days were up, I was transferred to another dressing station for inoculation. I finally ended up resting for three days at the horse lines, which was eight miles away. I went back up the line after a few days' rest.

Our boys went on a raid to Fritz's trenches the morning of April 28. The raid yielded two prisoners, despite having minor casualties. The month finally terminated with wet, sloppy weather.

On May 1 our casualties were light. During a raid we had two men killed and eight wounded.

On May 5 a single soldier was killed in Supports battalion.

On the night of May 7, we were relieved by a Scottish regiment from Palestine, and we went out for a rest at Gencourt. We are having lots of rain, and we are in mud up to our necks. But, what do we care as long as we were going out for a rest.

We left the trenches about 9:00 p.m. and after walking for some distance we got to the road. After hanging around for two hours in the miserable rain we got into trucks. We pulled out, packed in like sardines.

We reached our place of abode after traveling for about four hours. It was a delightful little country village, located in a pleasant spot. We had comfortable billets, and the weather was remarkable.

The first day out was favorable for sleeping. You still like to get your bearings, and see what kind of people live in the village despite the fatigue. Another important feature was to get a well-deserved feed of eggs. It certainly was appreciated to procure cultured new-laid eggs and fresh milk from the cow.

Our first day in this place was exciting, and the people soon knew that the 75th was in town.

The next day was a clean-up day for the troops. After that, the general routine of work started with football and baseball.

On the afternoon of May 19 we had our sports. The sun was nearly roasting us. Nevertheless, the men played well with the officers and staff in the games. It was a Company competition. I was attending the Company "B" game and they won by two points.

After the sports our football team had to play off a competition match with the 54th. The game had ended in a draw a few days before. After an hour of play, it was still a draw. Then on May 22, the game had to be played for a third time. This time the game was played on a different field four miles away.

Both battalions marched up to the field as a huge crowd from other battalions looked on as spectators. The whistle blew for the start, and some very fast play was witnessed. At half time no team had scored, and the 54th was betting plenty of money on their team.

The whistle blew for the next half. Then we saw some play. The 54th was driving for a goal. With ten minutes remaining, the 75th meant business. They drove down the field and scored the first goal. The boys just jumped for joy in the air because they knew it was a win for our side. The 75th tried hard to score again but the game ended in our favor 1–0. We marched off as the band played an old marching song. We had enjoyed a rewarding day of sport.

On May 24 "B" Company was having a hey day with the prize money. They had extra food, beer and a concert. Up until this time we had had fantastic weather. Badly needed rain was now falling.

On May 26 we moved back to Camblain-Châtelain, making it the third time and the people received us with open arms. This time Fritz flew over at night in his planes, bombing. The people had made dugouts in the hills. On hearing the bomb warning, they would flee from their beds. Then they would rush to the dugouts until the all clear sounded. Consequently, the single bomb dropped on the village resulted in no deaths.

On June 15 we held the division sports, and it was an exciting day. Sport started at 9:30 a.m. at Pernes near the hospital. Crowds of nurses were present, and the men had dinner and supper on the field. Our battalion would make three firsts, two seconds, and one third-place finish.

The day of July 1 was momentous for me. I was Corporal for the sports events, and the Duke of Connaught was present. The field was about six miles away so we were taken there in motors.

July 10 we had to move from Camblain. We started off at 7:00 a.m., and had to walk about four miles to Divion to entrain. We rode for about three hours. Then, we walked about another mile to the camp near a little village called Angin.

The men went into the line south of Arras July 11. On the night of the 13th, M. Lenard was killed and several wounded.

On July 16 we moved to Maroeuil where we had adequate billets. The town had a delightful river to swim in as well as a trout stream. Also, an old tannery was still in operation.

Thirty soldiers, including myself, were taken out of the front line on the afternoon of July 16. We were sent to a camp with forty other soldiers of the battalion to form a Reserve Brigade. Each battalion sent about eighty men. We arrived at 4:00 p.m. with no huts for sleeping. So, we had to put up sheets and sleep under them. One kitchen was established for two battalions, and I was head chef. It rained all day, and I had to cook in the open. So, I had one hell of a time. Also, we were near a lot of huge guns, and old Fritz occasionally would bomb us. It was not very healthy.

I had to have repairs on my teeth, so I walked into Arras on July 22. Although civilians still lived in various parts of town, they did not like to leave their homes. The reason was the fear of being blown up at any minute. Yet they took all kinds of chances.

July 31 we moved out of the line and walked back about ten miles to Wanquetin. During the walk I passed out for a while because the heat was so intense.

We stayed in Wanquetin for two days, moving out August 3 at 4:30 p.m. We rode motor trucks all night, not knowing our destination. Finally, we stopped at a château on a farm, and at a church. We had billets in the barns and sheds.

On the night of August 4, we started off again at 8:30 p.m. for another place called Herissart. Herissart is about five miles away. It was a very arduous march, and it was all uphill. At the end of the march I went into a barn for some sleep.

That same night at 10:30 p.m. we received battle orders. After falling into formation we set off on another extensive march, leaving our packs behind.

It is now raining. For one hour we transferred across country in the darkness, resting for a few minutes.

We started off again trudging up and down steep hills. We passed through forests and mud, falling all over the place as it was intensely dark. We had never before done such a march at night. Mile after mile every man endured until we reached our destination, Talmas.

The cooks made us all some hot tea at 10:30 a.m. Because of being haggard and footsore we soon bedded down and quickly fell asleep.

Altogether we walked about 22 miles. It was an exhausting march and a wet and muddy day. During the night we began another twelve-mile march, falling in at 9:30 p.m. We had to push on despite our exhaustion and reluctance. Passing through Amiens after five hours of walking, we arrived at Boves Woods. In the woods we had no shelter, but the trees were enough. We just slumped down and slept until 1:00 a.m. We did have tea, although it was difficult to get water. We had to walk three miles for that water! The same night I walked about five miles to a station called Salouël for reinforcements.

There were no reinforcements when I arrived at the station. So I just dropped down and slept until morning.

August 6—No reinforcements arrived as the morning dawned. I did see a young Belgiam woman who could speak English. Her name was Elza Depoorter. I told her I had not washed for two days. So, I asked her if I could go to her home to wash up, and have something to eat. She said, "Yes." While I was eating, I received news we had advanced five miles. We did continue to advance.

August 8—When I got back to the battalion, they had taken their objective, a town called Quesnoy, including a German hospital with all the nurses and staff. We lost several officers including Captain Cummings and Major Bull, two of our original officers. Nevertheless, our casualties were light with about twenty killed and seventy-five wounded.

The town we captured was full of goods and paraphernalia. The men had an immense time with what the German Head Quarter Staff left behind. Different kinds of foodstuffs were seized, including massive quantities of beer and wine. You could see the men rolling barrels of beer into safe places and enjoying themselves. Many trophies were found too. The Germans had their wind up, but their German bombs were mighty.

August 17 in the afternoon we went into the front line for another trip. We were in for seven days. We had old Hun guessing this time.

On the night of August 24 we were relieved by the French 123rd Regiment. We pulled out on the night of August 25. After a march of about fifteen miles, we camped in the woods. Soaked to the skin, we arrived about 4:00 a.m. in the morning. I was drenched through, but I just spread my sheet, slumped down and slept in the rain.

At 8:00 a.m. we had breakfast. We stayed there that day and pulled out about 6:00 p.m. We walked into a station called Longueau the next evening. The walk was about three miles. There the YMCA gave us tea, and we entrained.

We traveled all night and part of the next day. Then we detrained and got on lorries and rode for about twelve miles. We walked about two miles after that into the woods to rest for the night.

The next day at 11:00 a.m. we pulled out again. After marching about eight miles, we landed at the Huns' line. The area was where we had been pushed out of the Arras front.

On the night of September 1 we moved up to the assembly point. On September 2 it was over the top. The battalion was exemplary, capturing lots of prisoners, but we had quite a few casualties, about twenty-four officers. The attack was the hottest time in the line.

On the night of September 5 we were replaced. So we went back about ten miles and had a few days' rest. We have had to dig in and make homes for ourselves.

On September 25 we relocated to Bullecourt. On the night of September 26 we moved up the line for another attack. Our objective is Bourthes.

Cambrai fell on Sunday, September 30. On September 31, we moved back to St. Quentin. From St. Quentin we relocated to Y. Camp on Arras Rd. We stayed at Y. Camp for four days then migrated back to E. Court St. Quentin for two days. We then went to Bancourt.

On Saturday, October 19 we went on leave, which started at 9:00 a.m. I walked fifteen miles to get a ride in a motorcar to Agnez-Les-Duisans. Agnez-Les-Duisans was about twenty miles away. I stayed the night and got a train the morning of October 20 to Calais.

I arrived in Calais at 7:30 p.m. just as it started to rain. Despite the rain I still had a two-mile walk to rest camp, and I arrived there soaking wet. I then wound up sleeping in a tent that was not rain proof.

I boarded the boat the next day at 12:15 p.m., arriving in Dover at 4:00 p.m. I caught the train in Dover at 4:30 p.m. and arrived in London at 7:30 p.m. I then slept at the Maple Leaf Club for the night. The next day, I went to Cirencester and arrived at 1:35 p.m. I was happy to get home to see Auguster, Morris and Harold.

In November 1917, the German Commander von Ludendorff met with his key generals in Mons, Belgium. The war, he declared, would be won in a single decisive blow as early in 1918 as possible. Thus, the German spring offensive of March 1918 was conceived.

The aim of the Germans was twofold. They wanted to capture the strategically important area of Amiens, a vital rail junction, and to divide the Allied armies, weakening them to the point where a combined counterattack would be impossible.

*To diminish Allied strength was also crucial following the United States'
decision to enter the war in 1917. The German generals knew they could not
wait.*

*The difficulty about Flanders was the mud. It was impossible to undertake
heavy mobile operations in the north until the terrain dried up. That would not
happen until midsummer. Ludendorff could not wait that long.*

*Preparations, as usual, were methodical, thorough and well-concealed. The
best men in the German army, elite storm troopers—Stosstruppen—were concentrated in assault divisions. Lesser soldiers would suffice elsewhere.
Ludendorff assigned the attack to three armies, significantly Hutier's 18th, von
der Marwitz's 2nd and von Below's 17th. This way he had the veteran troopers
on each of his flanks.*

*While the Germans massed their troops for the coming 1918 offensive, Field
Marshal Haig felt compelled to extend his line southward to relieve the exhausted French.*

*Ludendorff's weapons would be mass and surprise. Operation Michael
would fall on the British. So would a second assault, when Operation Michael
had succeeded.*

*The attack was to center around Péronne, France. It would cover a forty-mile
front that ran from Arras down to the Oise River where the French took control.
The Huns were going all the way.*

*The Allies knew that the Germans would attack, but when the blow fell on
March 21, it caught the British 3rd Army and 5th Army by surprise, forcing them
to divide and retreat. The morning of March 21 was thick with fog, German
weather that grounded the allied planes. At 0440 hours the German guns
opened up, six thousand of them firing a saturation barrage on the British position. Precisely five hours later they switched to selected targets. Then grey-clad
German infantry emerged from the trenches and started forward.*

*Toward midday the weather began to clear, and the British got their aircraft
airborne. For the rest of the day the squadrons made valiant efforts to slow the
Germans down.*

By midday the allied commander Gough knew he was in real trouble. He had two divisions in his rear areas in General Headquarters reserve; he asked for them and got them. Immediately Haig gave two more divisions to Byng. By nightfall the news was either unfavorable or nonexistent.

An elated von Ludendorff poured in more troops. Now he was convinced that he could split the British from the French, and roll up Haig's army against the English Channel.

The morning of March 22 was foggy again, and the Germans kept coming. The sky cleared earlier than the day before, but the best efforts of the allied air squadrons still could not stop the German advance. By late afternoon the German commander Hutier had broken his men through into the clear. They had gotten past the last positions and were heading full-tilt for Ham, the Somme and the Canal du Nord.

Byng was still holding stubbornly in front of Baupaume, and von der Marwitz remained stuck in the deeper British trench system in the center. The French were sending up six divisions to help Gough.

Now the battle had imposed its own logic on Ludendorff. Instead of directing the attack to the northwest, he decided to go with Hutier's success and push to the southwest. His general target became Amiens instead of Doullens.

On March 23 Hutier's troops followed Gough's allied troops so fast that they captured bridges across the Somme before Gough's engineers could blow them.

On March 25, the 3rd and 4th Australian divisions were on their way, hastily instructed to plug the gap and to assist in stopping the German offensive.

On March 28, six British divisions astride the Scarpe River halted thirteen German divisions on their drive to Arras. To the west and south, the Huns pushed through the towns of Péronne, Albert, Montdidier, Noyon—to the edge of Villers-Bretonneux. In the short space of just over a week since launching the offensive, German troops were almost at the gates of Amiens. The Allies had to prevent the Germans from passing through Villers-Bretonneux, the main area before Amiens.

It was at this point that hunger, exhaustion, and the terrible casualties the storm-troopers had suffered from a shattered but unbeaten British army took its toll.

The British lost 163,500 troops. The French lost 77,000 men. The German losses were staggering too—239,000 Stosstruppen, *the elite of their fighting men.*

About March 29, Bert and the 75th battalion had been positioned to hold the line for ten days in front of Rocklincourt.

Thirty kilometres (nineteen miles) south of Rocklincourt and Arras on April 5,1918, Operation Michael petered out for the Germans. The Allies had not been split but united.

By July of 1918, the allied counteroffensive was in full swing. By July 11, the 75th was back in the line south of Arras.

The French General Foch looked over the maps and planned how he would fight the rest of the war. He produced a straightforward, no-nonsense scheme. Foch's plan had none of the frantic scurrying of Ludendorff's plans.

In August, 1918, Foch was appointed Marshal of France and Commander in Chief of the entire allied armies. Foch displayed a mastery of the art of war in coordinating the allied counterattacks which were crowned by the armistice of November 11,1918.

From August 8, 1918, to the armistice of November 11, the Canadians were in the forefront of the allied advance that finally defeated Germany.

The first stage was the clearing of three bothersome salients held by the Huns. In each case several ends were to be served.

On August 3, 1918, the Marne salient was pinched out. The Germans were back on the Vesle River, and there they stopped. The whole offensive action pro-vided the first bright spot on the allied horizon for the year. That same day, in late afternoon, Bert and the newly formed reserve brigade left Wanquetin, not knowing where they were going. Late that night they received battle orders. Under the cover of darkness an unusual sustained night march had com-menced. After about eleven hours they reached Boves Woods, thirty-four kilo-metres south of Herissart and about twenty kilometres south of Amiens.

Attention now turned to the Amiens salient. The conflict was to be a joint Anglo-French attack. The British on this front had seventeen infantry divisions. Significantly, of those seventeen divisions there were four Canadian brigades and five Australian brigades. Six hundred tanks, more than two thousand guns and eight hundred aircraft were assigned to give the seventeen divisions cover and observation. The French had eleven hundred aircraft and ten infantry divisions, despite having fewer tanks there. Against these twenty-seven Allied divisions the Huns could only muster twenty thin formations, a handful of tanks and fewer than four hundred aircraft. Their morale was weak, their units rotted with sickness, and their strength suffered from a slow but steady seepage of desertions.

To keep up the initiative, Foch's second blow to the Huns was soon to be delivered south of the Somme River on August 8, 1918. Most of the glory went to the Canadian and Australian troops in the attack. If a deadly breakthrough occurred, the Canadian Army Corps would be snatched from the Vimy-Arras front and moved south, prepared to cope with the enemy. The Canadians had received a special course of training back at Arras, even though the crisis had passed without having to use it.

When the time came for the attack on the Somme front, Foch gave orders for the strictest secrecy and for elaborate measures for deceiving the Germans. While the bulk of the Canadian troops were smuggled under cover of night to the Amiens region, some battalions were moved north to Belgium. They moved down roads in the middle of the day with colours flying and bands playing, and were put into the firing line near Mount Kemmel. Here telephone conversations were put on for the express benefit of the German listeners and enemy spies. Also, a few American troops and British shock troops went through movements suggesting an impending attack. Then, when the enemy was taking steps to meet a tremendous attack on the Mount Kemmel front, the camouflage troops were rushed back to their own units. The mighty drive up the Somme valley now began. Meanwhile, low-flying aircraft masked the sound of troops, guns and tanks moving into forests west of Amiens.

At daybreak on August 8, 1918, the Allies launched a counteroffensive. With no early warning, Rawlinson's British 4th Army plus the Canadian and Australian brigades walked forward into a thick dawn mist to attack.

The Germans were completely surprised and swept off their feet.

Bert had returned to his own 75th battalion, which meanwhile had achieved their objective by capturing the town of Quesnoy.

The tide was turning. Only the failure of raw, battle-weary French and British divisions on either flank limited the greatest single allied victory of the war.

By September 12, the Huns were losing ground much faster than they had gained it in the spring campaign. That day was made famous in history by the United States Army launching its first independent offensive effort—the elimination of the St. Mihiel salient, southeast of the Arras-Cambrai area.

The German withdrawal was still in progress when the US Army attacked on September 12. A secondary assault by 110,000 French troops took place three hours later. Over fourteen hundred aircraft under the command of General William Mitchell supported the advancing U.S. and French troops. On the first day the main attack advanced nine kilometres (5.5 miles) to reach Thiancourt and the French troops captured the village of Dommartin. By September 16, the entire St. Mihiel salient was under Allied control.

With the St. Mihiel salient destroyed, General Foch could now go on planning attacks on the all-important German lateral line of communication running through Sedan and Montmedy.

The closing days of September saw allied victories all up and down the western front. On the Cambrai front, the British advanced seven miles on a thirty-five-mile front (about twenty-two kilometres). In the process the British took twenty-two thousand prisoners and three hundred guns and reached the outskirts of Cambrai.

The outlook now became alarming for Germany. So, on Saturday October 5, 1918, Germany indicated to U.S. president Woodrow Wilson that the German high command desired an armistice. A peace conference was in order. The basis of discussion would be the fourteen points that President Wilson had pro-

posed to establish the basis for a fair and lasting peace following the victory of the Allies. Ultimately, Wilson was compelled to abandon his insistence upon the acceptance of his full program, but his fourteenth point was realized in the League of Nations, established as a result of the Paris Peace Conference (1919).

The U.S. urged Germany to be specific on what they wanted. In addition, the United States asserted that during negotiations, Germany conduct military warfare according to the laws of nations.

Foch's plan had been to deceive the Germans before that August 8, 1918, attack. Consistent with Foch's plan, Bert's reserve unit moved in cover of darkness from the Vimy-Arras region between August 4 and 7. They were prepared to fight in that final counteroffensive south of Amiens in case of a German breakthrough. They were not needed.

The period from August 8, 1918, to the Armistice of November 11, 1918, is known as Canada's "Hundred Days." General Erich Ludendorf, then Chief of Staff of the German army referred to August 8 as "the Black Day of the German army."

The Canadian losses between August 22 and October 11 amounted to 30,805 officers and men, far exceeding the losses of the Somme. Optimists took comfort; the losses paid for victories. Capturing Sancourt, located five kilometres (three miles) north of Cambrai, virtually wiped out the 75th (Mississauga) Battalion; only 78 of 467 men survived unscathed, but only 25 of the 389 casualties were fatalities. Nevertheless, Bert played a diversionary part in the allied offensive. Also, his unit helped ram through the southern part of the Hindenburg line east of Arras.

But the Germans were not finished yet. Why was it that Bert called them "those cursed Huns?"

The Duke of Connaught inspecting Canadian troops (middle foreground). (The John A. Hertel Co. Ltd., Toronto, 1919)

Marshall Ferdinand Foch, Commander in Chief of the entire Allied Armies. (The John A. Hertel Co. Ltd., Toronto, 1919)

CHAPTER 10

Those Cursed Huns

After all, what is there to gain for the blood that has been shed to satisfy the greed of the being called the Kaiser? ... It is true they were industrious and a hard-working people—also very clever ... They are now a beaten nation to be looked upon in the future as a savage race for the deeds done in Belgium.

Excerpts from a letter Bert Cooke wrote to his wife.

As a private, Bert's letters were censored. It is likely envelopes bore the official declaration "I certify on my honour that the contents of this envelope refer to nothing but intimate and domestic matters," which the writer had to sign.

The trust in the honour of other ranks was such that these letters were opened by the censors anyway.

The following letter is the last of the letters Bert wrote to his family.

To my dear wife and family, what does it profit a man to give the whole world nothing?

After all, what is war and the things gained by it? I for one think war is an awful thing in these enlightened days. Years ago, it was the savage people that fought each other for very simple things. But after years of education people would think little disputes could be settled without bloodshed. We were taught as soon as we were old enough to love one another and has that teaching been ground into us all these years for nothing? Can we say we love the Germans after what they have done? I often think, are we worshippers of the same God as the Kaiser and his people, or does their God teach them to kill and destroy and make slaves of the people as they like? What are we to believe? I thought the teaching of the Holy Book was for peace on earth and good will to man. But at the present time I think things have changed.

Also, another point strikes me. That is, we are fighting a Protestant nation and assisting Catholic countries, people that reject us at other times, but now is a different thing all together. They want our assistance. Now what can we make out of it all? For over two years we have been fighting and preparing for final victory and to my mind we are the people our God has stood by, and has given us good men, men that have brains to work with. We have lost other good men but today we are in a better position than we ever were in, and to my mind we are the chosen people to rule the world. We have no desire for war but when we are put to the test our men are second to none, and that has been proven in this struggle. After all, what is there to gain for the blood that has been shed to satisfy the greed of the being called the Kaiser? I suppose he had worked himself and his people up to such a pitch that they thought nothing on this earth could stop them, as they had the men and all the implements of war that was possible to make for a destruction of men and country. Also, God was their leader second to the Kaiser, but he hadn't thought of the English and their God. So, he started on a poor little country first and then his troubles began. We promised to stand by them and now was the time for England's little army to have something to say in the matter. At that very time, God our heavenly Father stepped in and worked a miracle. Only a few English soldiers stopped the German army from rushing through and taking France. Thus we learned at the very first that the God we have been taught to love stood by us and turned the wicked army that had been doing things that savages would not do.

Then, how can they be called a civilized people? It is true they were industrious and a hard-working people—also very clever. But, now what is our opinion of them? They are now a beaten nation to be looked upon in the future as a savage race for the deeds done in Belgium, and for that how could they expect to be treated as a Godly people? Then again, from land we turn to the sea. Have they acted like human beings? No, like beasts and wild ones at that! Oh, many a brave heart is asleep in the deep through their doggish tricks sinking ships with poor women and children aboard without the slightest warning.

Is that how their God has taught them? If so, He must be a peculiar person and not the same heavenly Father that we worship.

Fair play is the thing we are taught. If they had learned that, they would have brought their navy out and said now it is one thing or the other, the best man win. But, no! They only came out in parts and had to retire those that were left.

Also, another price of their barbarous work was sending the zips over to England to destroy women and children. All these things go to prove that they are a savage race and uncivilized and will be called such by all people in the future. Now, after all, what will be our gain? Some of our capitalists will gain wealth, but it is the people who will have to pay, what with taxes and cripples it will be more than some people will be able to stand.

Always bringing misery and poverty, but on the other hand this war was forced upon us by the people that will be always looked upon as murderers. But, we have a lot to be thankful for. Our people have been very patient and have trusted in God to guide our leaders, and help men to bear the burden they have to bear.

God knows how our boys in the trenches have had to suffer, especially in the winter with the cold and the mud and not the right kind of food for this weather. The summer is not so bad but it is the time when so many of our boys are laid away in their last resting place. Gone, but not forgotten. That is the time when it makes one think that war isn't worth the sacrifice when we go from town to town and see the soldiers' cemetery on the hill or in the valley, and filled with little mounds and a small cross at the head with the words, "Here lies the body of some mother's son who died doing his duty. Rest in Peace." Then I say, no war! It's hell and I often say to myself why does God allow all this? Perhaps He has a reason. He moves in mysterious ways, His wonders to perform. I hope and trust that He will work wonders before many more weeks have gone, and that the war will end before our brave men who are in the trenches are doomed.

We all want to see Germany crushed. That is so, but I hope and trust that something will happen that the struggle will be finished without much more bloodshed. We must leave it entirely with our Maker who has taught us to trust in Him, and He will never fail us. He has proven that on many occasions. My prayer is that God will protect me and help me to do unto others as I would like to be done unto, and then I won't be afraid to meet my Maker face to face when I have crossed the bar.

Bert

I started for Calais on November 6 and arrived at Somain at 3:00 a.m. the next morning. I stayed there and had breakfast, then started off for Denain. I reached there in time for dinner. Lots of civilians and the town was not damaged from the bombs.

I then went to the theatre this evening. The civilians, especially the women, were so delighted to see us. They wanted to kiss you all the time. I stayed at the rest camp for the night and then went on to Valenciennes.

The next day crowds of civilians were there and were delighted to see us. From there we were to be part of the Battalion at Anzin-Saint-Aubin. Here we had a furnished house. We even had beds for sleeping with white sheets on them. This place was immaculate. It would make your heart bleed to see some of the women cleaning up.

We started away from Anzin-Saint-Aubin November 14. It was a sight to see the civilians getting back to their homes on our way to Germany. People were carrying packs on their backs. Others had trucks filled with odd bits of stuff that had been saved. Yet others used small carts drawn by a milking cow, or an ox. It was like a circus but heart-breaking.

Countless numbers of old people are too weak to walk. So, they are being wheeled from place to place on an old truck. Drivers of our motor trucks were even told to carry civilians back from bondage to freedom.

In Belgium we stayed for five days in a town called La Louvière. During our stay we were treated like one of their own. They gave us wine they had hidden from the Huns for four years.

Those Huns would take anything they could get to make shells—even the brass knobs from the doors and stoves. So, we could tell that they were hard up for materials.

The people gave us the best rooms and the best beds in the homes as we were billeted in private houses. They were delighted to have us.

We left La Louvière for a village near Mons, but it was not as pleasant as La Louvière. It was a meager village, so we would journey into Mons. Mons was the bigger town and more fun.

Our old Colonel came back on November 24, and we welcomed him with a huge reception. We were delighted to have him back.

We left the little village on December 12. We started away at 8:00 a.m. and marched eleven miles to La Louvière, and it rained the whole distance. We were soaked to the skin when we arrived, but we had a fine billet. Four of us billeted in a massive house belonging to a gentleman. The people made us quite welcome. They gave us a bottle of wine and decent beds for sleeping. Also other people gave us wine and brandy, and we had a fun time around the town.

We pulled out at 8:00 a.m. for a place called Courcelles the next morning. It was a very grueling fifteen-mile walk, and it was raining again. Each village and town we passed through the people lined the streets giving us a friendly reception and treating us very well. I had a favorable billet, and a proper bed that was very pleasing.

In the morning I came downstairs to find my boots cleaned and coffee ready before breakfast. We started off again at 8:00 a.m. walking another eighteen miles. All along the route we saw German motor lorries left in bad shape with iron bands on the wheels instead of rubber. We arrived at our place of rest at 4:00 p.m.

The two thousand villagers of Monceau-sur-Sambre did not give us such an obliging reception. Even the billets were unreliable. Nevertheless, we were able to rest.

The next day we started off on another fifteen-mile march to a paltry village called Thorbais. We arrived there at 12:30 p.m. It rained heavily the whole fifteen miles, and we were delighted to get there. The people were much nicer, and the women were too. We billeted here in Thorbais, starting out at 8:30 a.m. the next morning on another march. We were now at the end of our trip for two or three days.

We were billeted in another little village. In fact, our battalion occupied five insignificant villages. I was in Gesves, which is about fifteen miles from Namur. They say we have to stay here for two months. Gesves is terribly quiet with nothing to do. We do not even have a place to go for fun. If we have to stay here for those two months we will all go dotty.

Because the area is a farming district, the people had to work hard for the Germans. The Germans forced them to plant their crops and then turn over all the harvest back to them. In addition, all the pigs, cows and poultry were taken from the farms. The Huns did not even pay the farmers a cent.

The people ate anything they could find to survive, even insects and maggots. So, we could tell they were desperate for food. We shared any food we had to spare with them. They enjoyed giving us coffee.

I was working for "A" Company and billeted in a modest farmhouse. The people were young and had a child. The man was in grave shape because of gangrene in one of his hands. But they liked seeing the Canadian soldiers.

The civilians told us some frightful stories all along the lines. They told us how the Germans would slice off the breasts from the women. Another place near here the Germans shot two hundred and fifty women and children. A person would hardly believe these atrocities.

In another town, all the civilians were put in a church with gasoline thrown in it and incinerated, all of them. In one of the houses a French soldier lay wounded on a bed. A German officer discovered him. The officer poured gasoline on him, burning him to death and the house. It was time the war had finished.

At 5:30 p.m. we had an excellent Christmas Day dinner. It was served to us in a huge granary. The men decorated the room, and the food was laid out in style. Every man had all he could eat of turkey, vegetables, and Christmas pudding. After breakfast every man received a new pair of socks, eight packages of cigarettes, and three packages of tobacco. Also, we received one orange and chocolates. We had lots to drink, and we all had a very exceptional time.

We were wasting time until our turn came to go back to the front line.

The last night in the old year was very dull. So, I went to bed at 10:00 p.m. and slept the old year out and the new one in.

New Year's morning was very bright. It didn't rain all day. So, the men took opportunities to go for walks. We transferred away from Gesves on January 4 at 6:30 a.m., feeling no remorse. Our destination is a tiny village called Longueville south of Brussels.

It was a difficult march, but the weather was fine. The cobblestone roads were abominable for marching because it was brutal on the feet.

In our last billets, the people were sorry I had to leave. They were up at 5:00 a.m. in the morning, lit a fire and gave us coffee. As usual, I had hot water for washing.

The man had killed a rabbit the day before. He wanted me to take the rabbit, and have someone cook it for a decent meal. Also, they gave me plenty of waffles to eat on the way.

The night before they provided me with a filling supper. They certainly were kind to me and asked me to come back and visit them.

We arrived at Lives, which was not far away. Compared to other villages Lives is not too shabby. But, beyond that we had comfortable beds for sleeping.

The next day we started off at 8:30 a.m. We arrived at noon after a wearisome march at a place called Dion Le Mont. There I found a satisfactory billet for my pal and me. Immediately the people gave us an exceptional dinner. The meal consisted of soup, potatoes, cabbage and bread. In addition, we had boiled bacon, which was quite filling. Also, we were provided a room warmed by a fire and comfortable beds for sleeping. It felt rejuvenating to be able to relax around the fireplace.

Dancing was the dominant sport on Sunday. So, since it was Sunday, all the people would flock to the dance hall.

The morning of January 6 at 7:00 a.m. we commenced our march. Our destination this time is a place called La Hulpe about ten miles south of Brussels. It is a pleasant part of the country to walk through— if we did not have to carry anything on our backs. It was up and down hills the whole ten miles, arriving at our destination at noon. We were billeted in houses.

While I was in town, I visited a shoemaker shop. The people are paying outrageous prices for repairs and new boots. The people of La Hulpe are very fond of dancing too. Every night they would be at the dance halls from 5:00 p.m. until 9:00 p.m. But, on Sunday they made it a feast and a day of sport for the young and old. In some halls the music consisted of two melodeons and a cornet. It was awful music, but the people jigged around and enjoyed themselves. The boys in our band took their instruments down and gave them a few tunes too. The people thought it was remarkable.

I left for Brussels on January 18, 1919, and returned back to England, then home. My tour of duty was finished.

After the fall of Cambrai the Canadians were moved north toward Douai, and commenced an advance in the direction of Valenciennes. On October 20, after a number of preliminary successes, they captured the large mining town of Denain.

Four days on the road brought the Canadians to Valenciennes, an industrial city that was key to the new German defense line. Five under-strength German divisions guarded the city. Two of the five German divisions faced the Canadians across acres of flooded land, the Canal de l'Escaut.

Haig had ordered an advance on Valenciennes for November 3. Canadian gunnery staff prepared an elaborate fire plan to give the Huns the illusion they were being hit by their own artillery fire.

At 5:15 a.m., the area around Valenciennes exploded in a deluge of fire. Heavy German resistance was encountered during the day's fighting, but the Canadians were in an ugly mood that day. Too many Germans surrendered, complained a diarist of the 50th Battalion, but "some very useful killing was also achieved."

That night, patrols of the 3rd Division crossed into Valenciennes and by dawn the Germans had left. Eighty men died and three hundred men were wounded in the reoccupation.

In nine days the Corps advanced thirty miles (49 kilometres).

From Valenciennes, France, the Canadian route lay to the Belgian border and the city of Mons. It was a country of rapid streams, hills, hedges and dense forests, ideal for tough rearguard fighting. Rain poured down on marching troops every day but one. As transports lagged behind, weary infantry had to carry all they needed, from spare ammunition and grenades to extra rations. Engineers concentrated on keeping three brigades of heavy artillery up with the Corps as backup for any rearguard combat. On November 4, the 3rd Division ran into the German rearguard at Vicq, France, near the Belgian border. On November 5, at the Aunelle River on the Belgian frontier, a Canadian division ran into stiff rearguard resistance too. After a brief set-back, the 85th Battalion forced a passage. On November 6, the 2nd Division took over the advance.

By November 9, two Canadian divisions reached Jernappes, outside Mons. Air observers and deserters warned of a real battle at Mons. On November 10, both Canadian divisions found hardened resistance. Fighting through the coal-fields south of Mons continued. German machine-gunners hidden at every tip, claimed 350 Canadian casualties, only a few of them mortalities. Another Canadian Division, in its approach to Mons, spent the day cautiously probing its way around the west side of the city losing 116 men to machine guns and a few shells. Late that night, companies of the Royal Canadian Regiment moved cautiously into the city. The Germans were gone.

The first troops to enter Mons on November 11, 1918, were the 42nd Royal Highland Regiment of Canada, the famous Black Watch. The group was the *bodyguard of Sir Arthur Currie. The Black Watch paved the way for Currie when he made his triumphal entry into Mons on the afternoon of November 11.*

The few inhabitants who were left came out and stared in disbelief. The mind and heart, for the moment, could not comprehend that the war might be ending. To the city of Mons, Sir Arthur Currie presented a Canadian flag tied to a lance. This flag now stands in a conspicuous place in the council chamber of the city hall.

That day at 5:00 a.m., the armistice had been signed, effective six hours later at 11:00 a.m. The fighting was over. The most important condition of the armistice provided for evacuation of occupied territory, including Alsace-Lorraine, within two weeks. However, another term of the armistice called for allied occupation of the left bank of the Rhine River. The Canadian Corps was chosen as part of the army of occupation. From Mons, the Canadian Corps advanced through Belgium and into Germany.

The war movement advanced at an infantry pace of three miles an hour. The Canadians out-marched their neighboring corps thanks to their engineer brigades. But everything seemed to conspire to hold them up. The Germans had emptied the country of food, demolished every bridge, ripped up every railway and mined every road. The crowds of civilians who cheered the Canadian infantry and gunners desperately needed food and medical care. The Corp's trucks, worn out from months of hauling heavy shells, occasionally faced sixty-mile (ninety-seven-kilometre) turnarounds that usually were limited to one-way traffic. Soldiers footsore and weary from forced marches cursed the staff for late and inadequate supplies. Currie, in turn, raged at "higher authorities" who had failed to plan.

The time limit for the Germans to evacuate Belgium and Luxembourg and Alsace-Lorraine expired November 27, 1918. All German soldiers not out of these regions by that time were liable to capture and imprisonment.

On November 7, 1918, Bert and what was left of the 75th Battalion became part of another Battalion at Anzin-Saint-Aubin.

From November 14, 1918 on, Bert and the 75th were part of the rear guard and the occupation of Belgium. The job of the 75th was to protect the Allies' main corps that was following the evacuating German forces. So, although the 75th remained in a back-up role in Belgium, the rear guard contributed to an uneventful German evacuation resulting in minimal loss of life.

The execution of Edith Cavell in 1915 by the Germans makes us readily believe the atrocities that Bert relates.

Miss Cavell was a British nurse who served at a Red Cross hospital in Brussels, Belgium. On August 20, 1914, the German army marched into Brussels. As the war went on and the Belgians continued to suffer increasingly at the hands of the enemy, Miss Cavell felt morally compelled to compromise her nurse's status of civilian honour. She became one of a growing group that aided both Belgians of military age and escaped allied prisoners to cross the border into Holland. Edith Cavell was arrested by the Germans on August 5, 1915. Two months later, she and thirty-four other defendants were put on trial. She was accused not of spying, but of "causing harm" to the German forces by helping allied soldiers to escape, and of related crimes.

Being a strongly religious person, she refused to lie even to save her life. She and four others were sentenced to death, but only two of those sentences were carried out: Miss Cavell and that of a Brussels architect. The American delegation, neutral at that time, tried to intervene, but their efforts were futile. Miss Cavell and the architect were executed by a firing squad on October 12, 1915. Miss Cavell's body was returned to England in 1919, and services were conducted with military honours in Westminster Abbey.

There are not many historical records or memoirs left by fighting men or others recounting their part in the "Great War." Because of this, World War I is slowly receding from the collective memory of today's society. We should be keen to preserve the few left; this diary is a legacy not just for the Cooke family, but for all the families of those who made the supreme sacrifice.

Edith Cavell, British nurse whose execution by the Germans shocked the world. (The John A. Hertel Co. Ltd., Toronto, 1919)

Memorial erected in Brussels to Miss Edith Cavell, who was killed by the Germans on October 12, 1915. (The John A. Hertel Co. Ltd., Toronto, 1919)

A view of Brussels, Belgium. (Milly Walsh)

General Tasker H. Bliss, former Chief of Staff of the United States Army. (The John A. Hertel Co. Ltd., Toronto, 1919)

EPILOGUE

After the war, in May of 1919, the 75th Canadian Battalion returned to Canada aboard the ship *Mauretania*. A month later, on June 28, 1919, the Great War came to an official end amid great pomp and pageantry in the Hall of Mirrors at Versailles, France, the very place in which the German empire had been proclaimed at the expense of France.

Its cost in blood and treasure had been hideous. Casualties, of course, are by their nature relatively impossible to measure. Some estimates of the loss in human lives put the figure at 13 million dead soldiers and 13 million dead civilians.

In addition, there were 20 million wounded soldiers, 3 million prisoners, 9 million war orphans, 5 million war widows and 10 million war refugees. In *all* major wars fought between 1790 and 1913, the dead numbered twice as many as were killed in those four years. The war's cost has been estimated at $332 billion.

All this agony and ordeal—this famine, disease, destruction, and death—was it worth it? Did it bring the stable peace? Did it make the world safe for democracy?

For a while it did. But, the collapse of the empires created a vacuum into which new empires—like Communism and Fascism—were to rush. The Treaty of Versailles did not guarantee peace and stability. Its inevitable effects were described by a wise American soldier, General Tasker H. Bliss (one of the American delegates to the Peace Conference), who said: "We are in for a high period, followed by a low period. Then there will be the devil to pay all around the world."

The post-war "boom" of the twenties was the high period. The "Great Depression" was the low, and the "devil" was even then walking ghost-like through the bleak barren streets of Munich, Germany. He was, in his own words, a "human nothing." He had been a corporal in the German army. He had been very courageous and won medals. He had been gassed and had lain half-blind in a hospital cursing the "cowards" whom he accused of "betraying" Germany. Now, in that fateful summer of 1919, he was nearly hysterical with rage and shame to hear of "the great betrayal," the Treaty of Versailles. Soon he and six other men would form the National Socialist German Workers Party and dedicate it to the creation of a new Germany more ambitious even than the fallen Germany of the Kaiser.

Out of the rubble of the First World War a new danger arose—the Nazi Party and its creator, Adolf Hitler.

APPENDIX

The home station of the 87th Grenadier Guards is located in Montreal, Quebec. It received designation as a regiment of foot guards in 1912. Its long history through variously named units dates back to an Army Order dated 12 March 1764, signed and sealed by Colonel Frederick Haldimand at Three Rivers, Quebec, raising the first Canadian military unit under the British Crown. This unit was designated 1st Company, District of Montreal Militia. In 1807 under The Honourable James McGill, it was redesignated 1st Battalion, Montreal Militia. Four companies of this battalion saw active service during the War of 1812. In 1859, the unit was raised to regimental status by order of His Royal Highness, the Prince of Wales (later King Edward VII) with the title 1st Regiment, Prince of Wales' Volunteer Rifles of Canada, and for some time it was the only Regiment in Canadian Service. The Regiment provided volunteers for the Canadian Contingents during the war in South Africa in 1899 and earned the battle honour South Africa, 1899 – 1900. In the First World War, the Regiment contributed officers and men to the 14th and raised the 87th (Canadian Grenadier Guards) and 245th (Canadian Grenadier Guards) battalions, Canadian Expeditionary Force. The 87th Battalion served in France and Flanders from 12 August 1916 until the Armistice and earned a total of eighteen battle honours: seventeen Honorary Distinctions, and Private J.F. Young was awarded the Victoria Cross.

Chapter 1

Salonika: A chief port in Greek Macedonia on the gulf of Thessalonica east of the Axios River Delta on the shores of the Aegean Sea. It was used as an Allied Base.

75th Canadian Battalion: The 75th, 54th (Kootenays) and 85th (Nova Scotia Highlanders) battalions were reserve infantry units of the 4th Division. The two main battalions of the 4th Division were the 102nd (Warden's Warriors, northern British Columbia) and the 87th (Grenadier Guards, Montreal). Major General David Watson commanded the 4th Division and made up the 11th Brigade.

Chapter 2

The Toronto Scottish Regiment was raised on 1 July 1915 as the 75th (Mississauga) Battalion, Canadian Expeditionary Force (CEF) by Lieutenant Colonel Samuel Beckett. Within three weeks over one thousand five hundred personnel had been recruited. By March 1916, the battalion was fully trained and sailed for Liverpool. Over five thousand five hundred soldiers served in the battalion during the First World War; one thousand and forty-nine were killed, including Lieutenant Colonel Beckett. The 75th Battalion CEF was awarded 16 battle honours, and Captain Bellenden Hutcheson, the Medical Officer, was awarded the Victoria Cross.

Chapter 3

Crewe: A railway town in the midlands near Coventry, England.

First Contingent: A quota of troops set up by the government to be a force of eighty-three thousand men that reached England soon after the outbreak of war in 1914. Unfortunately the loading of the transports was less than successful. Far too little planning had been done, and chaos and confusion were the order of the day as ships were loaded and then unloaded, guns were loaded with their wheels still on, taking up extra space; equipment might end up on the wrong ship, and in the end much equipment was left behind. It embarked at Quebec in thirty-one transports. By the third week of September the transport ships had been assembled and the process of loading began by September 27th. It sailed in early October 1914 as a convoy. It was in the thick of the fighting in the second battle of Ypres.

Salisbury Plain was the destination for Canada's First Contingent. By 1916 the Canadians had formed four divisions, with a fifth to provide reinforcements.

Second Contingent: Consisting essentially of the 2nd Canadian Division, this contingent of troops was offered by Canada on 6 October 1914, three days after the First Contingent had left, and was accepted by the British War Office at the end of the month. Recruiting, which began immediately, was brisk, particularly in the west. It left Halifax, Nova Scotia, for England on board seventeen ships, which sailed separately (rather than in convoy as with the First Contingent) in May and June 1915. In England it was stationed in the Shorncliffe area on the south coast until it crossed the Channel for France between September 13 to 17 and went into the line almost immediately. The infantry component of this contingent consisted of the following battalions: the 18th, 19th, 20th, 21st, 22nd, 24th, 25th, 26th, 27th, 28th, 29th and 31st.

22nd French Canadian Regiment: Part of the Second Contingent under the command of Major General Henry Burstall, the "Van Doos," were part of the 5th Brigade. The nickname was an English corruption of *Vingt-Deuxième,* stuck and became the informal title of the battalion. It survives in its present day incarnation as part of the Canadian Army Permanent Force, the Royal 22nd Regiment (or *Régiment royale vingt-deuxième*). It was the only French-Canadian battalion to serve at the front in the First World War and it remains the major French-Canadian unit of today's Canadian Army Permanent Force. Although many other French-Canadian units were raised, they all acted as feeders for this particular battalion. It gained a reputation during the First World War as one of our toughest and hardest-fighting battalions.

Chapter 5

Somme River: Arising in northern France near Saint Quentin, the Somme flows northwest past Amiens, and, after a course of 241 kilometres (or 150 miles), empties into the English Channel near Saint-Valery-sur-Somme.

Vimy Ridge: A strategic location about sixteen kilometres north of the town of Vimy in northern France. The high crest of the ridge, the part that counted tactically, lay between two river valleys—the Souchey to the north and the Scarpe seven kilometres to the south.

Chapter 9

Maple Leaf Club: An establishment in London, England, opened by Lady Julia Drummond for Canadian soldiers on leave and providing meals, baths and lodging.

MAIN BATTLES OF THE CANADIAN FORCES
AFTER 1915

Courcelette, September 15, 1916: Six Battalions of the 2nd and 3rd Divisions attacked the French village of Courcelette. Monquet Farm was taken by the 1st Division and several other minor gains were made.

Ancre Heights: Regina Trench saw some of the bloodiest fighting of the war before its capture on November 11, 1916, by the 4th Division. On November 18, 1916, the 4th Division captured Desire Trench, the concluding action that year by the Canadians on the Somme. Four thousand yards had been gained over a front of about three thousand yards with casualties amounting to twenty-four thousand all ranks by the 28th of November, 1916.

Vimy Ridge, April 9, 1917: During the winter months of 1916 – 1917, the Canadian Corps reorganized while holding the line. In preparation for the attack on Vimy Ridge, many small raids were conducted against the enemy.

One raid pulled on the night of February 28 – March 1 is today referred to as the March First Gas Attack. One thousand seven hundred men of the 54th, 72nd, 73rd, and 75th battalions lined the trenches awaiting the word to go over the top. There were fears that if wire-cutting torpedoes were employed, the enemy would be alerted. In place of the mechanical wire-cutting devices, clouds of poison gas were to be used to cover the attack.

The tanks of chlorine were opened, and the gas floated in the gentle breeze. As the Canadians started off, the wind changed and blew the lethal gas back into their own lines. As a result, both the attacking battalions (the 54th and 75th) lost their colonels as well as a total of 687 men. About thirty-five Germans were captured.

The enemy had considered Vimy Ridge to be impregnable until the battle with the Canadians on April 9, 1917. The French had tried to take it, losing upwards of one hundred and fifty thousand men in the attempt. The British then tried, but the Ridge still remained defiantly in the hands of the Germans.

On April 10, the 4th Division captured Hill 145, and on April 12, the 1st, 2nd, 3rd, and 4th Divisions captured The Pimple. Casualties for the three operations (Vimy, Hill 145, and the Pimple) added up to 266 officers and 9,700 other ranks. Other small battles and engagements were waged in the Vimy–Thelus trenches by the 1st and 2nd Divisions.

Fresnoy, May 3, 1917: During April and May, the Canadian Corps captured nine villages and a total of 5,000 prisoners, 64 artillery pieces, 106 trench mortars and 126 machine guns. In the early part of August, the Corps advanced toward Lens and the 4th Division captured Avion and La Couiette.

On August 15, the 1st and 2nd divisions, in company with the 4th Division, captured Hill 70. Battle was waged for ten days, and the Corps suffered ten thousand casualties during July and August of 1917.

Passchendaele, October and November 1917: In October, the Corps moved to Flanders to aid the British in their Autumn Offensive. The attack on Passchendaele Ridge took several stages to complete, and due to this careful planning, all objectives were carried. On October 22, the 3rd and 4th Divisions manned 2,800 yards of trench. On October 26, they attacked and carried Bellevue Spur.

In the first week of November, the 1st and 2nd divisions relieved the 3rd and 4th divisions and attacked and captured Passchendaele Ridge. Approximately two square miles of land was claimed, but the two months of action cost sixteen thousand casualties. During the capture of Passchendaele, forty-four enemy officers and one thousand two hundred other ranks were captured.

During the winter months of 1917–1918, the Canadian Corps held the line across a wide front near Vimy and the days were spent maintaining and repairing old trench systems and constructing new networks. During this period it was decided to use the newly formed 5th Division and maintain and augment the four other divisions at the Front rather than send it as a complete division.

During March of 1918, the Germans launched a final offensive in an attempt to break through the Allies and finish the war in complete victory. On April 24, the Canadian Corps extended until the four divisions covered a front some twelve kilometres long south of Lens. By the first week in May, the Corps, with the exception of the 2nd Division, went into Reserve. The 3rd Division relieved the 2nd Division about two months later. The Corps now moved to the vicinity of Amiens and prepared for battle.

Amiens, August 8 to 17, 1918: The Corps now held the centre of the British Front Line between Avre and Ancre. In an attempt which proved successful, the line was extended, and the Germans were beaten back over a distance of twenty-three kilometres. Amiens was saved—at a cost of 11,725 casualties. The Corps took an impressive total of spoils of war: 9,000 prisoners, 185 field pieces, 1,000 machine guns and 125 trench mortars.

Arras, August 26 to September 4, 1918: The Corps deployed along a front eight kilometres wide astride the Arras–Cambrai Road. The attack moved out on August 26. By the first of September, the 1st and 4th divisions took over the line and captured Upton Wood and the Crow's Nest. For the total actions, 11,000 casualties were suffered. Ten thousand prisoners and 100 artillery pieces were captured, along with 1,100 machine guns and 75 trench mortars.

Drocourt-Queant Line: On September 2, 1918, the 1st and 4th divisions captured Dury. By the next day, the Corps covered a front sixteen kilometres wide flanking the Canal Du Nord. The Canadians moved on and penetrated the Hindenburg Line, thus outflanking the Germans.

Cambrai, September 27 to October 9, 1918: In taking Cambrai on the ninth of October, the Canadian Corps suffered 18,000 casualties and captured 7,500 prisoners, 200 field pieces, 1,000 machine guns, and 30 trench mortars.

Valenciennes: This town fell to the 4th Division on November 2, 1918. About one thousand five hundred Germans were captured at a cost of approximately one thousand casualties.

Mons: On the last day of the war, the Canadians captured the Belgian town from which the British had been driven in 1914. One hundred prisoners were taken and seventy-five Canadians were reported as casualties. It fell to the 3rd Division to have the honour of capturing the city where the British and Germans first exchanged fire so long ago in 1914.

The 1st and 2nd divisions became part of the Army of Occupation, while the 3rd and 4th divisions spent the winter of 1918 in garrison in Mons and Brussels.

THE 4TH DIVISION

Commanding Officers

Brigadier-General Lord Brooke, C.M.G., M.V.O., November 19, 1915–May 11, 1916.

Major-General Sir David Watson, K.C.B., C.M.G., May 11 1916–demobilization.

Composition

12 Brigaded Infantry Battalions

Artillery

3rd Brigade, Canadian Field Artillery comprised of the 10th, 11th and 12th Field Batteries and the 9th Howitzer Battery.

4th Brigade, Canadian Field Artillery comprised of the 13th, 19th and 27th field batteries and the 21st Howitzer Battery.

Support Units of the 4th Division

4th Canadian Machine Gun Corps Battalion

4th Canadian Army Service Corps Divisional Train

11th, 12th, 13th field ambulances (Medical)

10th, 11th 12th trench mortar batteries (one per Brigade)

10th, 11th, 12th battalions, Canadian Engineers

4th Division Signal Company

4th Division Employment Company

75TH CANADIAN INFANTRY BATTALION

Mississauga Battalion

Authority: Go 103a of 15 August 1915

Recruiting Area: Toronto, Hamilton, London

Mobilization HQ: Toronto, Ont.

Service:

Canada—June 30, 1915—April 1, 1916

England—April 9, 1916—August 11, 1916

France—August 12, 1916—May 2, 1919

Canada—Returned aboard R.M.S. *Mauretania*

Commanding Officers

Lieutenant-Colonel S.G. Beckett, April 1, 1916—March 1, 1917

Lieutenant-Colonel C.B. Worsnop, D.S.O., March 11, 1917—April 16, 1917

Lieutenant-Colonel C.C. Harbottle, D.S.O., April 16, 1917—Demobilization

Battle Honours:

Somme, 1916

Ancre Heights, Ancre, 1916

Arras, 1917–1918

Vimy, 1917

Hill 70, Lens

Ypres, 1917

Passchendaele, Amiens, Scarpe 1918

Drocourt–Queant, Hindenburgh Line, Canal du Nord, Valenciennes, Sambre, France and Flanders 1916–1918.

BIBLIOGRAPHY

Baldwin, Hanson W. *World War 1: An Outline History.* New York: Harper & Row Publishers Inc., 1962.

Berton, Pierre. *Vimy.* Toronto: McClelland & Stewart Ltd., 1986.

Craig, Gordon A. *Europe Since 1815.* New York: Holt, Reinhart and Winston, Inc., 1961.

Duncan, S.J., and W.M. Clark. *The Pictorial History of the Great War.* Toronto: The John A. Hertel Co. Ltd., 1919.

Gilbert, Martin. *First World War Atlas.* London, England: Weidenfeld & Nicolson, 1970.

Goodspeed, D.J. *The Road Past Vimy: The Canadian Corps, 1914–1918.* Toronto: Macmillan of Canada, 1969.

Keegan, John. *The First World War.* Toronto: Key Porter Books Limited, 1998.

March, Francis A., PhD. *History of the World War.* Brantford: The Bradley-Garretson Co. Ltd., 1918.

McWilliams, J.L., and R. James Steel. *The Suicide Battalion.* Edmonton: Hurtig Publishers, 1978.

Meek, John F. *Over the Top! The Canadian Infantry in the First World War.* Orangeville, 1971.

Morton, Desmond, and J.L. Granatstein. *Marching to Armageddon: Canadians & the Great War 1914–1919.* Toronto: Lester & Orpen Dennys, 1989.

Morton, Desmond. *When Your Numbers Up: The Canadian Soldier in the First World War.* Toronto: Random House of Canada, 1993.

Parkinson, Roger. *The Origins of World War One.* East Sussex, England: Wayland Publishers Ltd., 1970.

Santor, Donald M. *Canadiana Scrapbook: Canadians at War 1914-1918.* Scarborough: Prentice Hall of Canada Ltd., 1978.

Stokesbury, James L. *A Short History of World War One.* New York: William Morrow & Company Inc., 1981.

Stromberg, Roland N. *Europe in the Twentieth Century, Fourth Edition.* Upper Saddle River, New Jersey: Prentice Hall, 1997.

"The Times History of War Illustrated, Volume 6." *The Times.* London: Printing House Square, 1916: 196.